sex you!

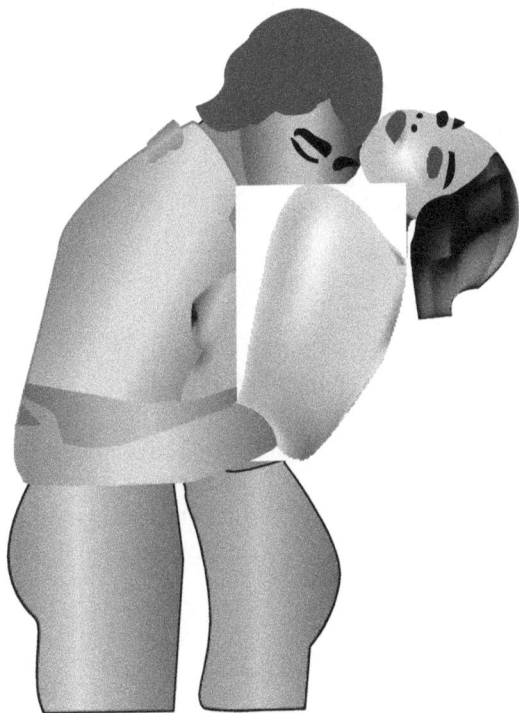

Michael Beloved

sex you!

Proof-reading Editor:
- Marcia Beloved

Cover Art + Final diagrams:
- Michael Beloved

Graphics Consultant:
- Sir Paul Castagna

Financial Outlay
- Śrīman Prem Vallabha

Correspondence:
Michael Beloved
3703 Foster Ave
Brooklyn NY 11203 USA

Email:
axisnexus@gmail.com
sexyoumail@gmail.com

ISBN
978-0-9819332-4-5
LCCN
2010901772

Table of Contents

Introduction

This book is about where we came from and where we will transit to. This pertains to what happened before birth and what will occur after death.

This is not a religious discourse. This deals with psychic facts. In the physical world we are confronted with certain realities, some of which we can do nothing to stop. It is the same in the psychic world.

After forty years of minute observations of subtle existence and its effects on physical existence, I share discoveries and insights. Neither birth nor death is mysterious and religion has no monopoly on either factor. For centuries humanity was bogged down by pastors, priests, shamans and the like with various superstitions regarding the cause and operations of human birth and death, as if those incidences are any different for the animals and vegetation.

After reading this book you should be able to figure out how you got this body and know what you will be doing and where you will be going when you are permanently separated from it.

sex you!

For Bimby, Baapo, Oakie and Bokey, some of my ancestors who resurfaced on this side of existence, after a span in the astral world, where they were lost due to not having any idea of how to fulfill desires in a subtle dimension.

And to their material sponsors, Marcia Beloved and Sharon Thornton.

Om Namo Shivaya!

Chapter 1
Passage through the Father's Body

Components of romance

Sexual expression concerns the life force, not the intellect, not the soul, not anything else. If the life force is controlled, sexual complications could be regulated efficiently. The encouraging power of ancestors who require rebirth, surfaces in our awareness as romance. The particular ancestor involved may not be conscious of the desire for birth, but would be conscious of an enthusiasm for getting into this world. In our psyches, that enthusiasm is interpreted as a flow of sexual pleasure. It increases in intensity until semen is emitted from the male body, hopefully not to be wasted but to enter into a female body for implantation in a womb.

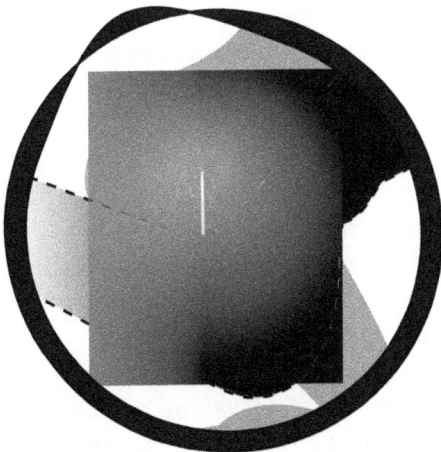

In that sense, the embrace of male and female lovers is more or less the eagerness of a departed ancestor to get into the woman's body to be implanted into her womb.

During conception, the lusty influences are a combination of these forces:

- *the male*
- *the female*
- *souls in subtle existence who require bodies*
- *the focus of supernatural beings who tally births and deaths.*
- *the permitting interest of providence*
- *the social environment.*

The male is the entity who plays the part of an implanter of sexual fluids. That person is assisted and prompted by the life force within his body. Without this life force, the male could not participate since he would have no impetus or arousal. In homosexual relations the one who penetrates is the male involved. In lesbian relationships, the male-profiled female performs that function.

In either heterosexual or same-sex relationships, disembodied entities are involved. It is a fact, however, that disembodied souls acquire bodies only when semen is transferred to a female body. In semen transfer into an anus or in an oral transfer, frustration and disappointment are felt by those disembodied persons who endeavor for baby forms.

In same-sex relationships, the entity trying for rebirth is frustrated repeatedly. In that sense, same-sex situations are non-productive and cause anguish on the psychological plane for the disembodied persons involved. They experience the frustration of repeatedly being displaced from spoilt semen.

In a lesbian relationship the situation is more complicated, in that a female has to take the aggressive part as an emitter of sexual fluids and in that interaction there is stimulation of sexual areas to bring the female body to climax. Disembodied souls enter that female form, mistaking it for a male one. They force that body to act as if it were a male one. The situation is such that women who are possessed by these ancestors acquire artificial male organs. Using these gadgets they act the male part with another female.

In heterosexual relationships, the male and female partners, though predominant on the physical side of existence, are the least significant part of a sexual relationship. They are instruments of the process. If they are successfully victimized, they become parents. If through contraceptive methods a pregnancy does not develop, they may experience emotional complications as a consequence of depriving ancestors of infant bodies.

Souls in the subtle world who require bodies, provide the major portion of the impetus for romance and sexual pleasure. The psychic energy of such souls, their enthusiasm for physical life, contributes to the intensity of sexual affairs.

The soul enters the semen of the father and lives in a

sex you!

liquid body as sperm. Then that soul is transferred in a rush of energy into the mother's womb for further development to change the liquid into a developed fleshy body.

Before attaining the present body, we were reduced to such an extent that we entered a miniscule sperm particle. We travelled through tubes in the sexual apparatus of the father's body before entering the mother's uterus and penetrating an egg in her womb.

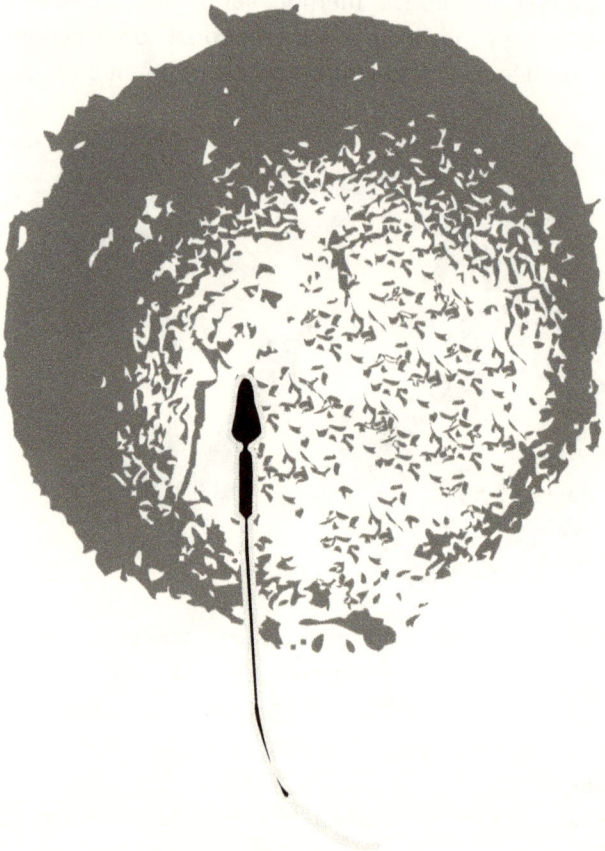

Mystics in India, wrote in the Upanishads, that the spirit's core is as small as one ten thousandth ($\frac{1}{10,000}$) of the tip of a hair. It is microscopic at the core, though expansive in capacity. As such it can enter a sperm. It is so supernatural that it can enter a thought or feeling in either of its would-be parents.

The disembodied soul who is transferred to the mother's body is not particularly conscious of its movement from a man's testes to a woman's womb. Still, its energies are involved. It experiences the transfer as an enthusiasm to get something it desires.

As for the souls who require rebirth, there are millions and trillions of them. If anyone is given the chance to be a human being, it would take the opportunity without hesitation. The human form of life is so special, so desirable, that entities requiring rebirth would take a body even from enslaved parents. They would take a deformed body, a retarded or diseased one. In fact any type of human body is rated as being better than any other life form. There is desperation on the astral planes among those who require human forms. Hoping to get embryos, they rush here and there whenever they sense sexual

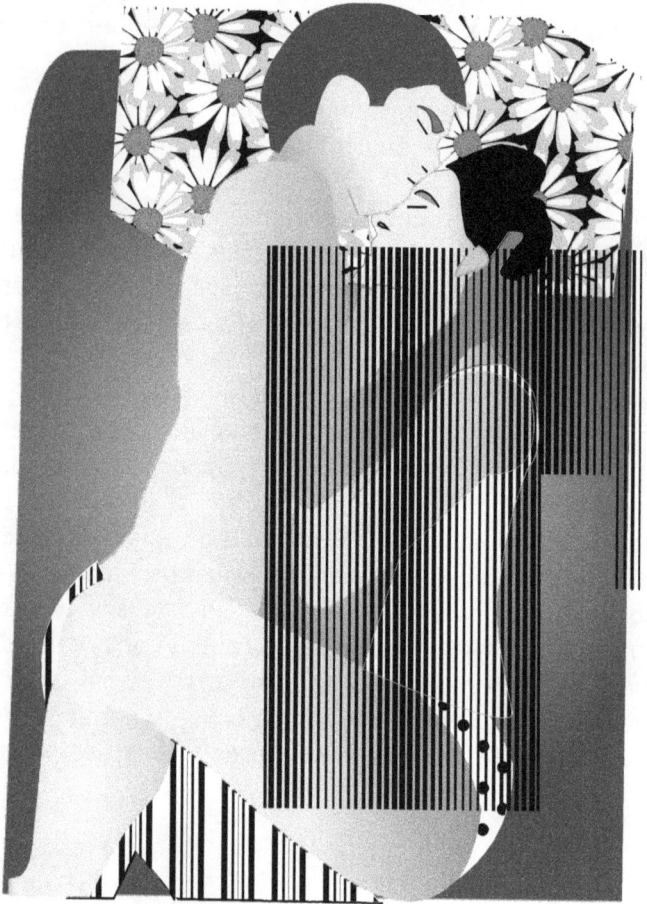

activity.

There is a range of supernatural personalities who are not the Supreme Being. Even though they are not members of Godhead, they have broad powers to monitor entries into and disappearances from the subtle world.

One such person, the deity of affection, regulates emotions. He induces couples to take responsibility for progeny. He fuses affection into the psyche of reluctant humans. Enthused by feelings of love, the victims participate in acts of sexual contact through which progeny is produced.

By using contraceptives, humans may circumvent the power of this deity. However, such actions may provoke reactions in the life to come, where one might be required to stay on the ghostly level in want of a body for some time. We, who abort children today, may be aborted in the future. And we, who enjoy sex without begetting, may, after departing the present bodies, enter the sexual feelings of lusty human beings to be enjoyed without getting the benefit of an embryo.

There is a deity who directs the rebirth of the disembodied souls. This person assesses the recent life activities of a departed person and recommends an avenue for rebirth. Sometimes this deity arranges the arrest of the subtle body of a departed soul and sends that person for a limited time to a hellish place. When the soul is released from hellish circumstances, the same deity arranges rebirth in a human or animal body which matches the person's sensual profile.

Many entities who committed criminal acts, escape being arrested by this deity. They dodge ghost police by taking shelter in the emotions of friends and family. Eventually they fuse into someone's affection and enter bodies of persons who live on this physical side of existence and who are obligated to them for services rendered in previous lives. If no one is found who is obligated, they enter into the body of any person who is sympathetic to their life energy. This is, of course, a supernatural process. We experience it as moods. These mood energies penetrate us as nice feelings and as desired ideas.

In a spiritual manual titled *Bhagavad Gītā*, Krishna said that the soul carries different ideas of life from one body to another, just as the air carries aromas. By our

sex you!

conception of life and our elevating or degrading habits, we take a new body with a certain type of nose, tongue, eye, skin and ear, which is operated through the mind.

Thus we crave particular sense objects according to the sensual profile.

A living entity does not take birth merely by desire, or merely by divine intervention. Instead rebirth happens on the basis of those combined forces. Much is involved in one's rebirth. One's desire and tendency are factored in. The view of certain deities is regarded. The permissive or restrictive will of providence is applied. Social influences play a part as well.

On the social level, there is constant pressure for sexual involvement. This demand comes from relatives, friends and others whom we meet casually in the course of life. Disembodied entities who are desperate for physical life switch from one would-be parent to another in the urgency to get human forms. Thus if one meets a sexually-inclined man or woman, it is possible that a disembodied soul within that person's psyche, might switch over to one's body. This attracted entity would inspire one in sexual activity in the hope of assuming an embryo body. In the hereafter, there is a rush for the opportunity to develop new bodies.

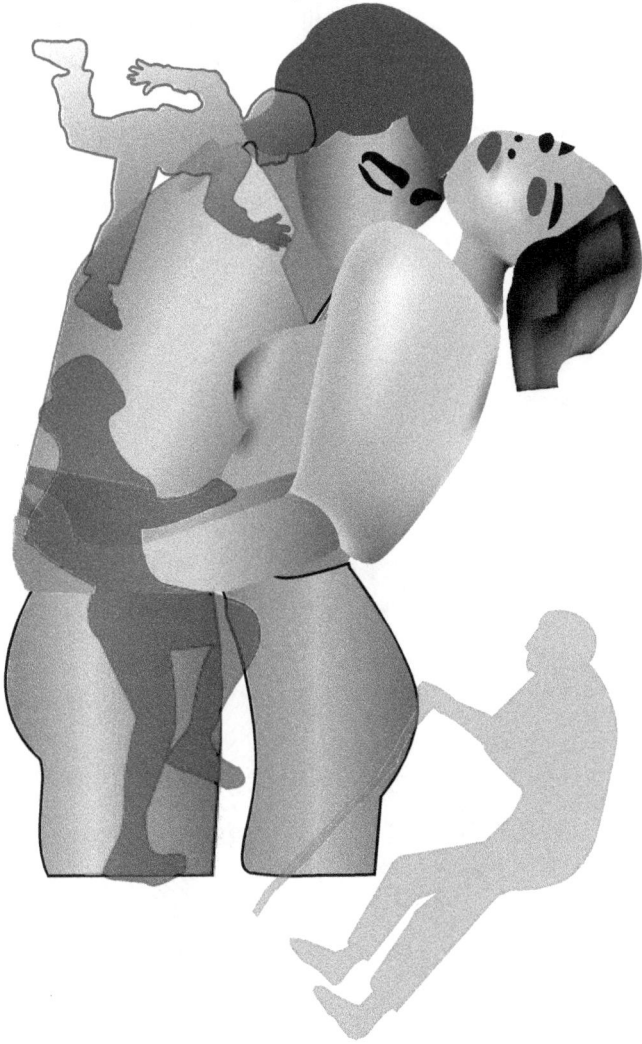

Romantic influence of disembodied souls

The life force is a psychic power generation system which is in the human psyche. It is sometimes called the kundalini, shakti, chi or psycho-nerve force. In humans, it

sex you!

is energized by breath, as well as by psychic energy from the astral world. This life force is a major contributor to the sexual process.

Romance is the influence of ancestors who require baby forms and who encourage a human male to beget a child in a female. The same type of pressure is applied in the animal kingdom.

Disembodied souls trying for rebirth easily enter into the bodies of their descendants, but they may enter the bodies of others as well. Emotional openness is the only prerequisite for such possession. And such openness might occur in the mind of a morally-upright person. It might occur in the mind of a priest who took vows for sexual non-participation.

The disembodied souls direct our senses to pursue the sexual interest of others. Despite moral views, still on occasion, one's attention is forcibly drawn to the sexual organs of others. This occurs especially through the visual sense. The mind forcibly moves the head and directs the eyes to the sexual organs of others. That mental force is so powerful that on occasion, religious people view explicit sexual scenes. They do this involuntarily, being forced by subtle pressure.

But why do the disembodied souls direct our bodies sexually?

What do they hope to achieve by continually bringing sex to our attention?

The answer is that they express sexual influence because we are hesitant to fulfill their need for bodies. They remind us by showing a sexually-attractive or provocatively-dressed human. The disembodied ancestors hope to achieve baby forms by encouraging thoughts of sexual union.

There is a related story in the *Mahābhārata*, an ancient text from India. Jarat was a wandering ascetic with aspirations for sex control. He viewed sexual companionship as a hindrance. Once he entered a cave and noticed some ghosts in astral bodies. He saw some disembodied men, but it seemed to him that they were assuming the form of bats. Surprised, he said, "Who are you? Why do you hang upside-down in this dark place?"

They replied, "We are in search of Jarat. If you find him, say that his ancestors will soon fall headlong to death in this cave."

When Jarat noticed these fellows in miniature forms, they hung from a braided cord while a rat stood on a ledge and gnawed on the strands. Jarat questioned the hung persons about the rodent. They told him that the cord symbolized time. The rat symbolized time's consumption. The interpretation was that if they did not acquire human bodies in the nick of time, they would be forced to assume bodies in an undesirable species.

Jarat identified himself as their descendant. They asked him to take a wife. So this is the idea. Sexual encouragement comes from the ancestors who need material forms.

The result of unimpaired sexual intercourse is progeny. The departed ancestors are the ones who use the sexual avenue to get embryos. Generally the living entity enters into the feelings of the would-be mother or father, according to which parent is more receptive to its energies. From there it enters into the bloodstream. If it enters the mother's emotions, it is transferred into the father's feelings through an emotional exchange where the father is influenced into accepting the energy vibration of the departed soul. Once the entity is in its would-be father's feelings, the father only perceives a feeling, emotion or thought.

From the subtle body of the would-be father, the entity is transferred into the bloodstream of the father's physical body.

After entering the bloodstream, the disembodied entity travels to the genitals, from which position it takes possession of semen and gets familiar with the father's genetic energy. After passing through the testes, where semen is manufactured, the living entity becomes eager to leave the father's body and so it travels to the seminal vesicle, which is inside the father's body in the pubic area. From there it urges the father repeatedly, until it is dispelled from his form.

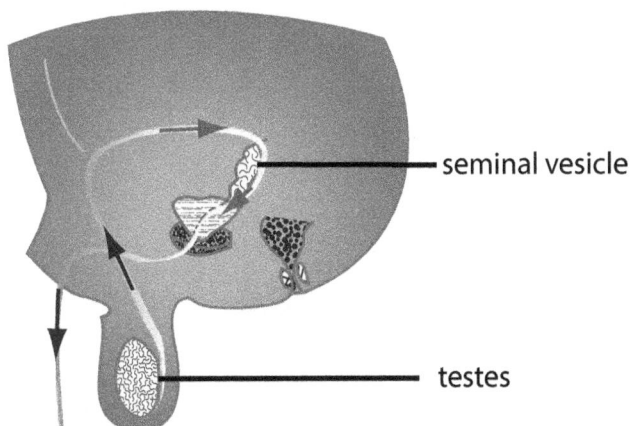

seminal vesicle

testes

sex you!

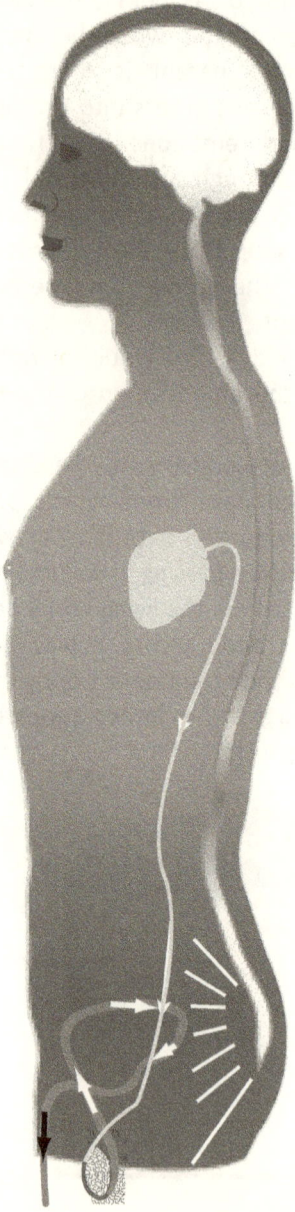

The disembodied entity is conscious of these travels through the father's subtle and gross bodies, but it interprets the travel as an eagerness for life only and not as a journey through tubes in a man's body. It experiences this as closeness to the father, as being in touch with someone it likes and needs. When it is expelled in sexual excitement it experiences an eagerness to be near the mother. When the father feels intense sexual pleasure, it is experienced by the disembodied entity as an urgency to move towards the pleasure center of the mother.

Chapter 2
Power Base
of the Ancestors

I will list some factors which give the disembodied souls leverage. These are avenues through which they enter our bodies with or without consent, regardless of whether we recognize the entry or not. They are facilitated by:

- *ancestral piety*
- *ancestral fate*
- *our fondness for sexual pleasure*
- *our identity with passion*
- *our lack of psychic insight*
- *our inability to assess social consequences*

Ancestral piety

Ancestral piety is the aggregate energy of ancestors' social contributions to human society in past lives. For instance, one's school teacher has piety or credits in one's life and can, on that basis, require of one, an infant form. One's grandparent or guardian has similar rights to enter one's body for the development of his or her new body.

Abortions and the numerous other methods used to prevent pregnancies are an effort to circumvent the system of allowing the ancestors unencumbered access to birth. With contraceptives we deny the ancestors the right to a new body but the story does not end there. Even if we successfully enjoy sex without begetting progeny, still we may face reactions hereafter. We may enjoy sex without producing children now, but what will be the outcome when we permanently leave our bodies? How will any of us acquire the next body? How will we process resentment from ancestors whom we deprived of a body?

Some young women desire to keep their bodies in a youthful condition. They may not want their abdomens to be distended by pregnancies. They may desire to maintain slim waists and non-sagging breasts. They may never consider that when they needed the present bodies, some other females sacrificed bodily contour on their behalf. Now their ancestors are in the astral planes in a crisis, rushing from one sexual scene to another, and being frustrated repeatedly as their seminal bodies are killed by poisonous vaginal creams; spoilt in condoms; spilled in anuses and wasted on the outside, instead of inside, a woman's womb.

Some males have sexual intercourse with women and make certain that no children are produced, thus giving themselves the presumed advantage of not having family responsibilities. Other males select males as sexual partners, just to be sure that pregnancies would never occur. However, their situation in the hereafter and in future lives may not be favorable. One who has a body now may be unaware how that body was acquired and may overlook or take for granted the nurturing contribution of the parents of that form.

The piety of the ancestors is potent stuff. It is such a powerful energy, that it forces us to have sexual intercourse even if we do not want to. In the desperate situation of needing a gross body, any living entity will trade piety or any psychological item he or she has, to get a birth opportunity.

Ancestral fate

Unless they are allowed access by providence, the ancestors cannot use their piety energy to motivate sex in the physical world. There is a legend of a deviant priest named Ajamil. He deviated from pious life when he associated with a prostitute. With his religious life in shambles, he was condemned in the community as a debauchee. He had children by the prostitute and had his fill of sexual excess. During the last moments of his life, he became perceptive of ghost police, who came to arrest his subtle body. In fear he tried to reach his son but he was unable to before his subtle body was seized. In the hereafter, the dream form or subtle body, which seems non-existent now, is felt to be realistic indeed. The ghost police with their strong subtle bodies pulled Ajamil's dream form out of his dying physical form. In the meantime, wanting to escape capture, he unsuccessfully tried to move into the body of his son. This is a case of an ancestor who was prohibited from using his piety to transfer to the body of a descendant.

Providence may or may not permit the entry of a disembodied soul into a relative's body, but usually fate is permissive of this. If, for instance, a certain ancestor is allowed, he or she will repeatedly pester the descendants. The ancestor will keep trying until there is an opening for pregnancy.

Our fondness for sexual pleasure

Our fondness of sexual pleasure is the one factor which keeps us generating progeny. It is such a powerful force that it blind-sides us to discretion. Essentially we are pleasure seekers. Most people want sex pleasure but not the responsibility for children. Still, their attitude towards the generation of children changes as soon as they lose their material bodies. When one finds oneself in the hereafter and discovers that one has lost the body and desires to be in the physical world, one encourages the generation of progeny.

Our identity with passion

Passionate beings take to human life on an earthly plane while the advanced beings take to the heavenly worlds or celestial regions and the mentally-sluggish, ignorant beings take to the animal world and even lower species. Most human beings are addicted to passion; the elevated ones become detached from passion. The passionate nature is itself a cause of susceptibility to the reproduction process and to sexual urges.

Our lack of psychic insight

Lack of psychic insight is costly to human beings. What transpires in the astral world would be of no consequence to us, if such affairs did not affect us. Our ignorance, in terms of not recognizing when we are affected, is a problem for us. This lack of insight relies on suppression of psychic tendencies. It is also due to persistent focus on physical things.

Our inability to assess consequences

The lack of moral values used to contribute to worldwide population expansion through sexual intercourse, with many pregnancies out of wedlock, but now through contraceptives, medically-supervised abortions and other related techniques, the population is effectively suppressed.

This situation does not serve the ancestors as well. Their efforts to get bodies through casual sexual relationships are frustrated by contraceptive usage or abortions where their sperm bodies or partially-developed fetal forms are killed.

Nullifying actions

Here is a listing of the power bases of the disembodied souls through which they enter our moods, to induce sexual activity. In this list I give methods of curtailing or nullifying these influences. Where no remedy is possible, I note that as unalterable.

Power Bases of Disembodied Souls	Nullifying Action
Ancestor's piety	-Repay them in another way -Direct one's children to provide bodies for them
Ancestral fate	-Cannot be altered by human beings
Our fondness for sexual pleasure	-Support moral principles -Absorb the influence of exalted souls who are morally-inclined most of the time
Our identity with passion.	-Abandon vulgarity -Take advice from godly persons
Our lack of psychic insight	-Read spiritual manuals like Bhagavad-Gītā -Associate with advanced mystics -Practice meditation
Our inability to assess social consequences	-Learn about the benefit of moral behavior. -Be aware of the immediate and long-range degradation produced by irresponsible acts

Once a person passes from a material body and transfers to the astral planes, needing to come back to this world, that person tries to contact relatives and friends in an effort to return to this side of existence. This contact is realized by us as thinking of a departed ancestor and having feelings of concern for the said person.

sex you!

Whatever good acts that person performed during the earthly life becomes a means of paying for the new birth. Such a person in that crisis, needing a physical body and feeling scared and uncomfortable as a ghost, will barter the record of services performed as the exchange for a baby form.

If a human is contacted by any such departed soul, he or she may divert the person by making an offer. One may explain that one will try to get another relative to beget the required body. Either one begets the body or one finds someone to do so. That is the procedure. Ignoring that departed person, denying him or her a birth opportunity, will bear unfavorable reactions, but if one offers the parenting services of another person, that promise must be validated.

I will give a personal experience. After begetting four children, a girl, a boy, and two girls in succession, I decided to cease reproduction. Still, I was consciously and unconsciously harassed by ancestors who required bodies. I rejected their demands for fulfillment of obligations due to services they rendered in past births. In addition, I was pressured by ancestors of my spouse. Her ancestors stressed that since their descendant served as the mother, they should be allowed to take birth. However, the author resisted because he found family obligation to be a drag on spiritual interest.

Family life significantly reduces the time one can devote to spiritual practice. Still the obligation remains. After all, if one needs a body, one needs one. It is as simple as that. Anyone who needs a body is in an unsettled state of mind. If it takes years to acquire an embryo, the anguish is unbearable. For instance, my eldest daughter was my paternal great grandmother in her immediate past life. She waited in the astral planes for about 15 years before getting her present body. She acquired that body through the piety placed in my life by her daughter.

Many departed souls in the astral regions are in uncomfortable positions. For them, getting a gross body is the priority. If one can beget a form for any such person, one renders a great service, especially if one can complete the responsibility by childhood training. The ancestors feel that contraceptive and abortive procedures should be avoided at all costs. So long as we are on this side of existence, such procedures are convenient, but as soon as we are displaced at death, we will be in the situation of the departed souls and we will readily understand their predicament.

Besides begetting a body, there are other ways of repaying an ancestor, but these other means are not of importance to the ancestor unless the said soul can get an infant body. In some cases one may promise to give the person involved an education if that person gets a body and reaches one as a student.

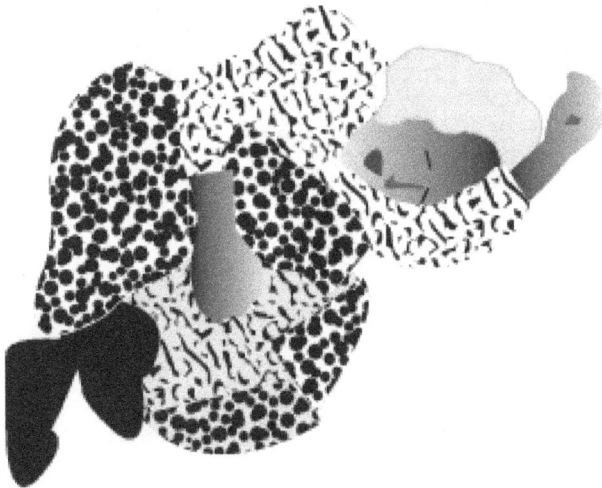

Elderly woman with terminal illness

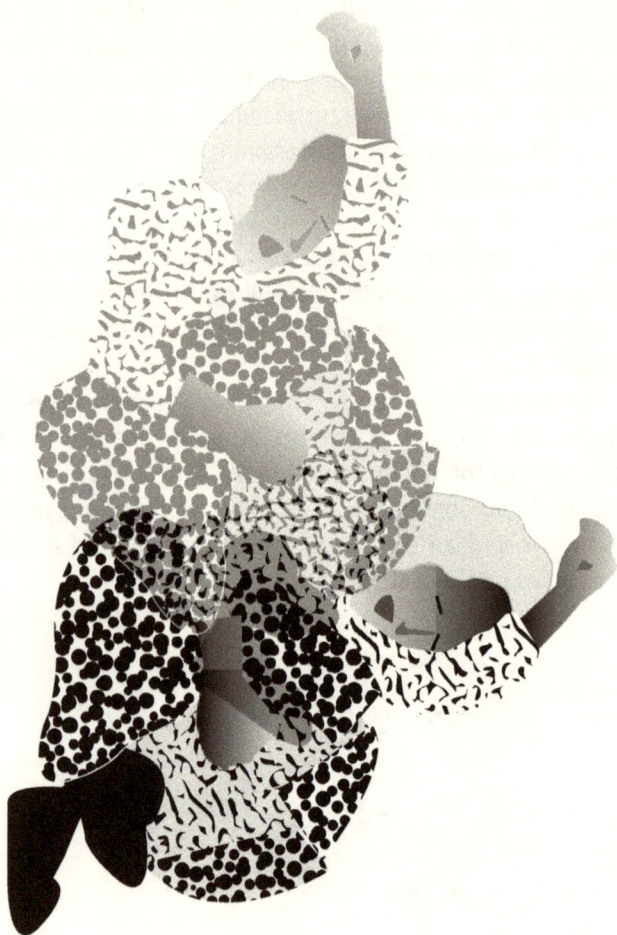

Subtle body separates as gross body dies

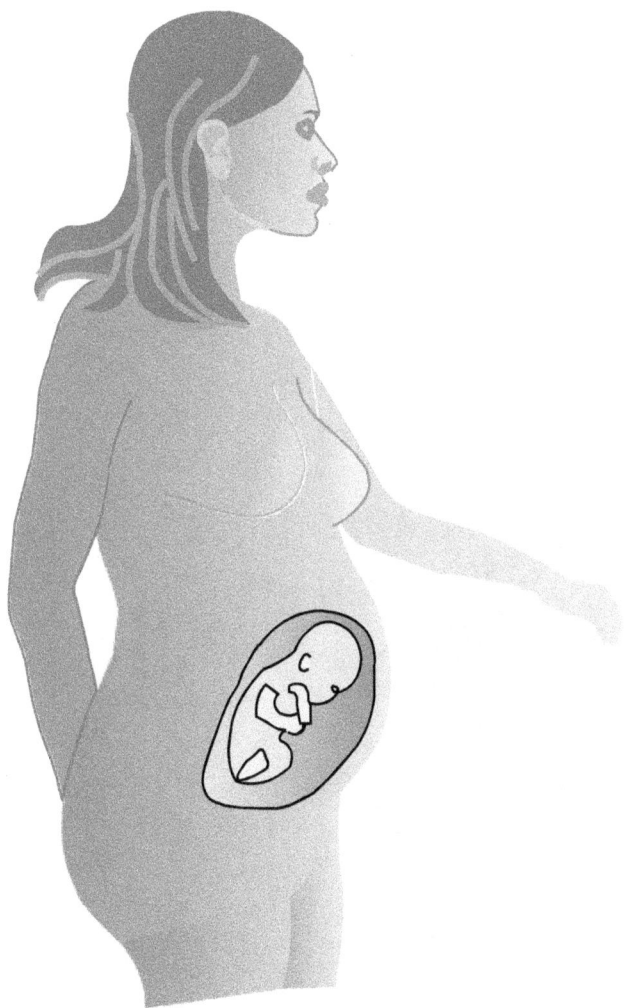

*Subtle body converts to an embryo shape
and becomes the child of a descendant*

New body as an infant

Ancestor as juvenile (right) getting education

Influence of a departed soul

I listed the disembodied entities as a main force of lusty energy within the gross body. Now I will elaborate. First of all, the disembodied entities affect us from within our bodies and from within the bodies of others who use gross forms. For instance, if one has no sexual considerations, sexual thoughts might arise if one is open to energy from a sexually-excited person. One does not have to know the person. Any subtle connection, even a glance or thought, may cause a transfer of affections.

The disembodied entitles who are in a someone's lusty energy exist there with gross and subtle impact on the person. Gross impact is felt as physical sex urge and urge for romance.

The disembodied souls first enter our feelings, our emotional and compassionate nature. From there, they enter the bloodstream. From the bloodstream they journey through the body and enter the genitals, and from there they await an opportunity to develop embryo forms. Perception of a disembodied entity's entry into our feelings is desired. If we can recognize the entry we may do something about it. If we are oblivious, we will mistake the sexual urges produced as our own and may become a victim of either masturbation, casual or criminal indulgence.

Do we ever stop to realize that if a pregnancy develops from a rape incident, someone benefits through that criminal contact? Someone benefits from prostitution if the lady becomes pregnant. That someone is the disembodied entity who gets the embryo body.

Some years ago, my mother passed from her gross body. When she first departed, she did not realize that her body was dead. She repeatedly tried to awaken up as her old body, as one instinctively does early in the morning to awaken physically. However, after trying to do this for three months, she began to conclude that something was amiss. It took her that length of time to realize this because her subtle body closely resembled the gross one she used. After realizing this, she approached me. I explained that her body passed on and that the body she used in the dream state was a subtle one.

She asked if there was any way her body could be re-awakened. I explained that it was impossible. She then requested a baby form and I said, "Yes, that is possible, if you can find a parent to produce it. I cannot help on this occasion. If you need a body and cannot get one, then later, one of my children may beget one for you."

Hearing this she was disappointed considerably and without speaking she thought, "Why should I wait to get a body? I am eager to live again. I hate being a ghost. I can feel myself but I cannot see this subtle form. I wish to be human again."

She went away to stay in the minds of other relatives. They experienced her as memorable thoughts. They called me to speak about her. They had fond memories and related this to the writer occasionally.

About one month later, she returned. By this time, she was accustomed to subtle existence. Still, she desired an earthly form. She therefore disregarded all previous explanations and exerted psychic power to force me to engage in sexual intercourse.

Ghosts are acutely aware of psychic influence. Since disembodied souls cannot act in the gross world, they focus their energies along psychic channels. My deceased mother began to exert tremendous influence on my body.

In influencing me for sexual affairs, she entered my emotions and forced my eyes to see the sexual areas of women. Such areas are the breasts, waist, shape of buttocks and indentation of clothing in the pubic area.

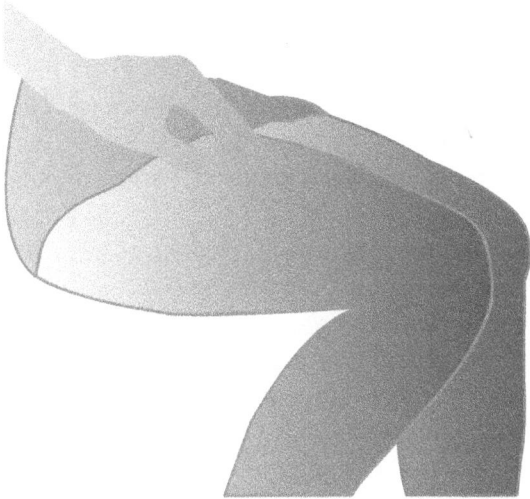

After this she began to transmit ideas of sexual pleasure, in the hope of getting the writer to recall such enjoyment. Since the writer was aware of the influence, he resisted. Readers might find this story to be incredible, but let us not forget that the mother of a body knows that body to an extent. The body of a son is genetically similar to that of the mother. Thus it is not amazing that a departed mother can enter the body of her son. She is familiar with the genetic pattern of her son's body which was produced from her last form. Her influence could saturate his body.

Disembodied entities in the gross and subtle bodies of others

We are also affected by disembodied entities who have pious credits in the lives of others and who affect us through friendship with others. This affection comes to us through attachments. Sexual, romantic and even friendly attraction forms a passage for the transmittance of lust.

Disembodied souls pass into our bodies through a flow of emotion.

Here is a list of relations and acquaintances who may cause transference of lust to one's body:

- **Conjugal relation:** *wife, girlfriend, husband, boyfriend*
- **Female relative:** *mother, sister, grandmother, aunt, daughter, niece*
- **Male relative:** *father, brother, grandfather, uncle, son, nephew*
- **Acquaintance:** *friend*

The wife or girlfriend, husband or boyfriend, can be a source of lusty desires leading to approved or criminal sexual contact. It is not unusual for an entity to first enter the feelings of a wife and then be transferred to the feelings of a husband to enter the husband's bloodstream and seminal fluid and then be re-transferred to the wife's psyche.

If a disembodied entity finds that a man is resistant, that entity may influence the man's partner and through the man's attachment, the entity will pass into his body effectively transcending his objection.

We may consider a child's influence on parents. If, for instance, the father is strict, the child soon senses that and learns to influence the mother. Once the mother agrees, the infant may induce her to change the view of the father. Before they become children, disembodied entities exert similar influences on their would-be parents.

Extra-marital lovers of any gender, are also sources of sexual energy transfer. In a monogamous society, a married man who contacts a girlfriend and has a sexual relationship with her, had better let that romance remain a secret, otherwise he faces certain disapproval. However, if he meets that woman and only flirts with her, or if he meets her and has sexual contact only on the subtle plane, no breach is detected. But in that case, if the subtle energies reflect into his gross body, he might have to play out the sex with his wife physically. She, in turn, may not realize that he acts out love for another woman.

This applies to women as well. Let us take, for example, the case of a woman who was attached to a certain boy during school days. After she marries another man, she may, on occasion, remember her fondness for the other male. That memory may be followed by dream contact. In some cases, there might be sexual contact in the dream association, but the woman may or may not be aware of it.

She may live out the sexual contact grossly with her husband. He might assume that her sexual performance is an indication of love for him. Actually, in that event he is in illusion, because it is an expression of her affection for the other man. A child may even be produced through such a relationship and the husband might never realize that the child was derived from the subtle energies of his wife's lover, and is an ancestor of that other man.

Disembodied entities who are in the feelings or thoughts of one's mother, sister, grandmother, aunt, daughter or niece can easily be transferred to one's body, regardless of whether one is aware of the transfer or not.

One can pick up sex desires from male relatives. The disembodied entities who reside in their emotions can easily be transferred into one's form and thus induce one to engage in sexual intercourse. Any living entity who requires a human body, will take a chance for birth here or there. A disembodied soul may have a preference of who should be its father, but in the final analysis, it will take an alternate parent. Any type of human body in any race, is better than an animal form. Instead of waiting patiently for years, to get the body one desires, one may settle for less and take a body through other human beings who carelessly engage in intercourse. In the desperation of trying to get a baby form, a person who had a white-skinned body in the past life and who was prejudiced, may take a black-skinned one. One who was in an ethnic group might take a body in another hated ethnicity. It is possible. Inasmuch as persons leave their native country and go to foreign lands in search of better living situations, so the disembodied souls would enter anyone's subtle body in the hope of a birth opportunity.

Any friend can serve as a point of transmittance of a disembodied soul into one's body. It does not matter if the friend is righteous or criminal. So long as the friendship is there, the lusty transmission can occur.

Disembodied entities in the atmosphere (ghosts)

At any point in time, there are millions of disembodied entities in the atmosphere. Normally we call these entities ghosts or spirits. The fact is, however, that any person who cannot get a human body and has to wait for days, weeks or years in a shifty, wavering astral existence, is a ghost. Generally we think that ghosts are evil but there are different types of ghosts, differing from ill-willed to mediocre to beneficent.

Any of us can become a ghost, depending on the form assumed after death. Generally we think that there are ghosts and there are human beings, and that ghosts haunt human beings. However, it all depends on location.

Disembodied entitles can enter one's body at any moment. Take for example the case of a man who meets a sexually-attractive woman on a lonesome street. All of a sudden, that man who had no previous criminal record, gets the idea that he should have sexual intercourse with the said lady. Under such circumstances, it is quite likely that he was possessed by a ghost who inspired the desire.

Chapter 3
Life Force

Excitement City

Sex desire is mostly traceable to other living entities. The main force is those who require rebirth. As long as we are on this side of existence, we may dismiss the idea of disembodied souls, but as soon as we depart from these bodies and have a need for new forms, we will be in the listing of the ghosts.

In some cases one traces a sexual energy long after completing an impulsive sexual act. It may take one, two or three days before one can definitely verify a sexual trace. Usually one has a dream or encounter in which one meets the party involved. Then one feels a lusty exchange which corresponds to the experience. At that point one can realize the influence. By this system one learns to recognize that a sexual impulse which may not be traced initially, can be identified thereafter.

One should realize that there is a difference between the body, the life force and the personality. Sexual drive is driven by the life force, which is known as the kundalini energy or as the psycho-nerve system sustaining the body. An allegoric tale about a king sheds some light on this. Once, a certain King Puran was wandering on this planet, trying to find suitable companions and accommodation. He searched for some time, unsuccessfully. Eventually he came upon a city in the Himalayan foothills. It had a nice lay-out, in his opinion. The city had nine gates. It was suitable for leisure and enjoyment. This particular place was called Excitement City.

King Puran was relieved to find this place, because he was tired of searching for a residence. The city had many accommodations with spacious air-cooled buildings, parks and fit residences. The only problem was that at first the place seemed to be vacated. In any case, Puran was hopeful that he would meet other human beings.

As he strolled here and there, he found a botanical garden. There he saw a sexually-attractive young lady and his joy knew no bounds. He noticed that the lady was followed by ten servants. Each of the servants had hundreds of assistants. Strangely, the woman was protected by a five-headed serpent.

Puran assessed the situation, for he could see that even though the woman's servants had spouses, the woman herself lacked a husband. She was young and beautiful, and like him, she appeared anxious to find a mate. He evaluated that though a virgin, the woman was sexually mature. Approaching her, he questioned.

She explained that she had no knowledge of the geographic location; nor did she have any idea who produced her; nor could she tell the names or backgrounds of the servants that accompanied her. And for that matter, all she knew was that the servants were loyal and the snake remained awake always to protect her.

She offered services. She invited Puran to be her companion for one hundred years. The lady said,

"O sweet man, I will arrange this city of nine gates for your satisfaction. Live here with me for one hundred years. All your desires can be fulfilled in this place. Just see how fortunate I am to have met you. After all, you seem capable and intelligent. You glance at me in a flirtatious way. I sense that you would be expert at sexual affairs. Let us join in matrimony, love one another and enjoy this desirable place.

"I feel that nothing is better than the union of a man and woman, especially the sexual connection which gives intense pleasure. I heard that cohabitation is not only pleasing to the participants, but also to the forefathers, the supernatural beings, the intellectual community, and just about everyone else. People appreciate an action which sponsors family responsibilities. And besides, there is the intense pleasure of sexual union, which results in pregnancies."

That proposal pleased King Puran. It was beyond his wildest dreams. All anxieties about finding a companion and country vanished from his mind. He unhesitantly coupled with the lady.

The story continues but I will explain the symbolism thus far. The place itself, Excitement City, represents the human body, which is a facility used by Puran, who represents the disembodied soul. The woman said it was a special place because the human body affords more variations of sexual enjoyment than any other species. In her view the human body afforded the special delight of sexual indulgence. Other creatures have sexual contact, but it is regulated by hormone cycles. The woman considered that human beings could enjoy sex regardless of nature's rhythm. She explained that the forefathers and others very much appreciate when a man couples with a woman and becomes attached to sexual pleasure.

The woman represented the analytical intelligence in every life form. The five-hooded snake represents the life force in the body. The ten servants symbolize the five senses and the five sensual objectives.

Puran, the king, is the transmigrating soul. It wanders hither and thither in various life forms of which the human species is the most preferred. At one time, Puran got lucky. He found Excitement City which represents a human embryo. When he entered the city, he became happy because in that situation, there were exciting affections between his mother and father.

Puran considered the human form to be especially affordable of sexual enjoyment, but he needed the cooperation of a queen and servants. In other words, unless we have the analytical intelligence and sensual facilities, we cannot operate a human body or any type of creature form for that matter.

However, the problem is that the life force is sexually-inclined and the intellect is ever-occupied calculating sexual opportunities. Therefore if they are not controlled and restricted, one will make no spiritual advancement. One will merely contribute to survival of a species.

Puran lived in that city with the cooperation of the queen. On occasion, he hunted animals outside the city. Whenever that happened, the queen became lonely. When he returned, she chided him and deprived him of sexual enjoyment. The idea is that if one misuses the human form by too much activity, it becomes tired and one cannot enjoy to the fullest. For instance, if one has too much intercourse, the life force terminates the enjoyment and one has to wait a day or two to allow the sexual force to recharge. In the meantime, one feels deprived. One's instinctual intelligence feels baffled and depressed.

Eventually, however, Puran was forced out of the city, or in other words, his body died. The life force, the intellect and the self reluctantly depart from a sick, dying body. When the gross body dies, the life force must leave it. That life force is a psychic phenomenon. Because of the life force's absence on this side of existence, persons here, say that one has died.

When one hundred years expired, Puran, the queen and servants, along with the city's protector, the five-hooded serpent, were forced to leave the city. They were arrested and dragged out by an enemy army which set fire to every part of the city. Puran, his wife, her serpent guard and servants were regretful of the incidence.

The enemy soldiers closed the higher gates of the metropolis. Puran and his assistants had to leave through the lowest gate which was the only one left open by the enemy. Everyone, even the serpent, was chained and dragged out by enemy soldiers. The reptile was fatigued because without Puran's or the queen's assistance, it fought the enemy day and night for one hundred years.

The explanation is that an unregulated pleasure-seeking life causes ill health in the body and through that, the higher faculties of the body, malfunction. In addition, there is eye disease, ear infection, heart disease, kidney failure, along with breathing problems aggravated by lung malfunction. Gradually the living entity is left only with one working part which is the anus. At the time of death, the soul and the psychic facilities loose contact with the body while taking shelter in the heat at the rectum. Since he was addicted to sexual pleasure, Puran's life force always remained focused in the lower part of the body, at the genitals and anus.

The mind of a living entity pervades the brain of the body, particularly in the frontal lobe. The life force, however, lives in the sacral region. In a woman's body sexual fluids develop into eggs which are in the lower belly. The eggs travel into the uterus which is in the same general area. Therefore the life force is friendly towards these energies which are located in its proximity. In a male, the sexual fluids are created in the testes which hang between the thighs. That fluid is then transferred into the seminal vesicle which is in the pubic area inside the body.

bladder

passage of semen

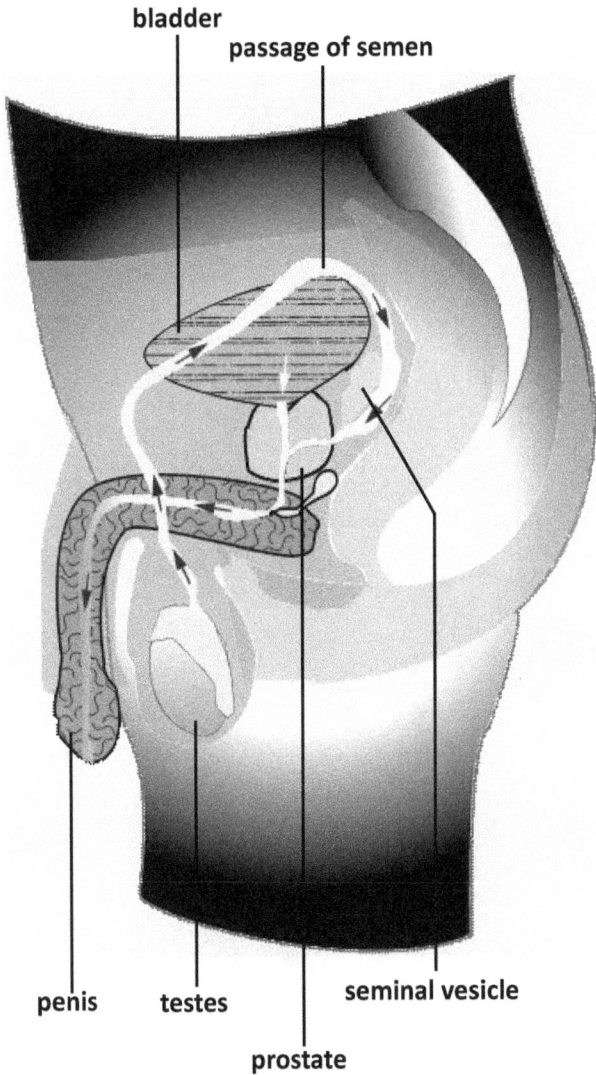

penis   testes   seminal vesicle

prostate

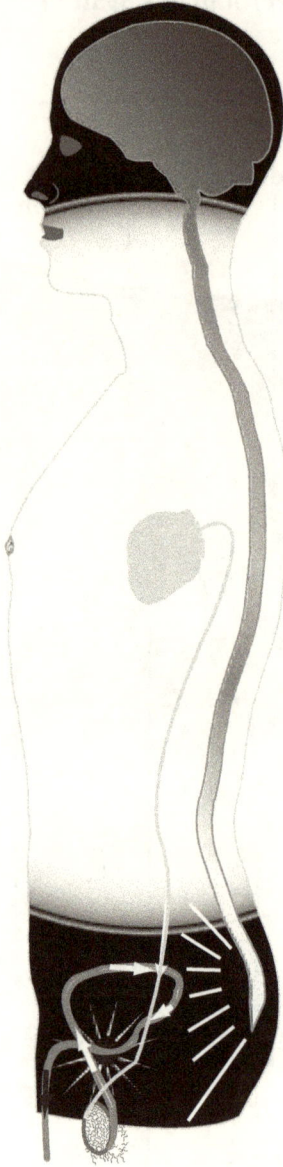

Female Reproductive System

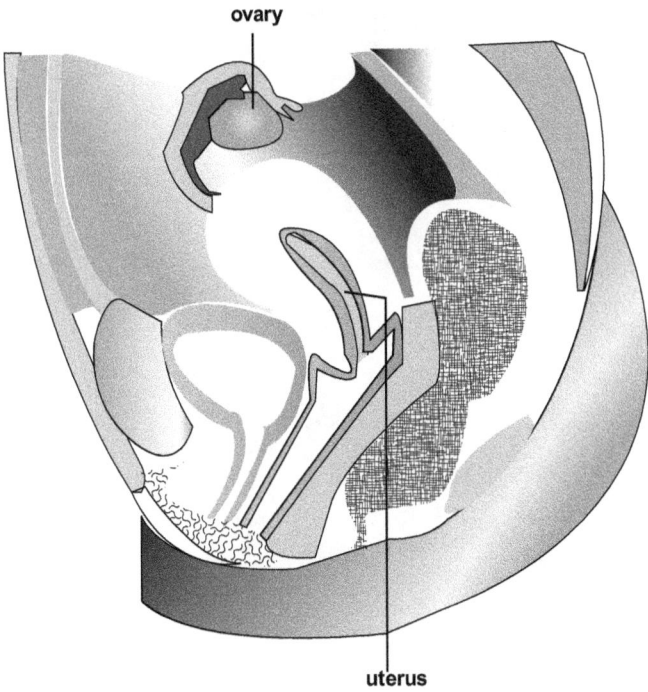

ovary

uterus

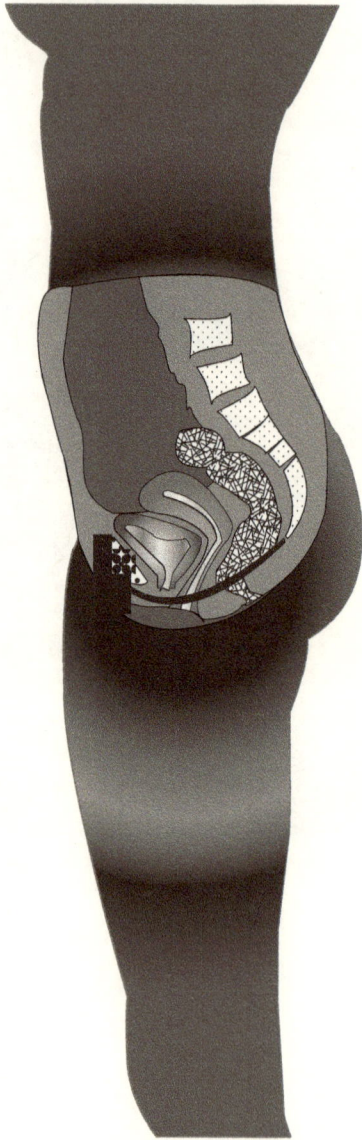

Types of semen

The life force is attracted to sexual fluids. If the fluids are stored in the seminal vesicle or uterus, the life force stays there to be in its association. The life force is not concerned with our status as cultured or vulgar, transcendental or materialistic persons. So long as sexual fluids are stored in the pubic area, the life force will be focused there, no matter what, and it will promote indulgence to discharge the liquid.

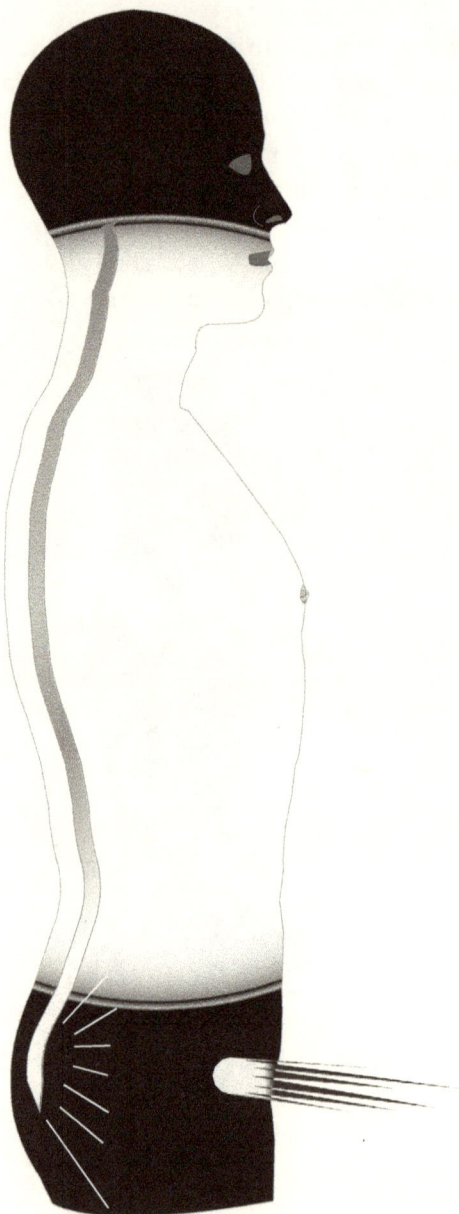

If the reproductive fluids moves up through the bloodstream and circulates through the body, the life force moves around the body along with it and produces a healthier physiology.

If the fluids moves up the spinal column and enters the brain, the life force does the same.

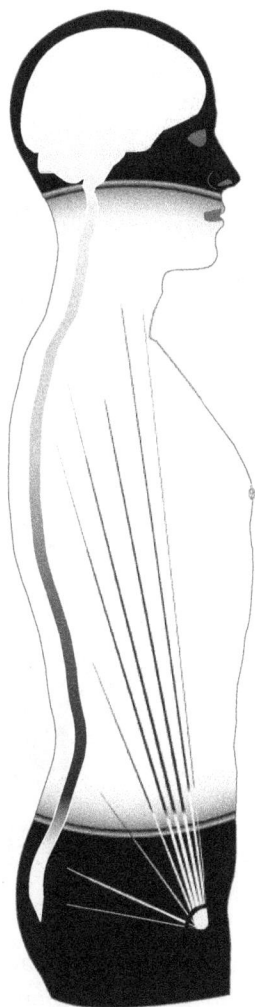

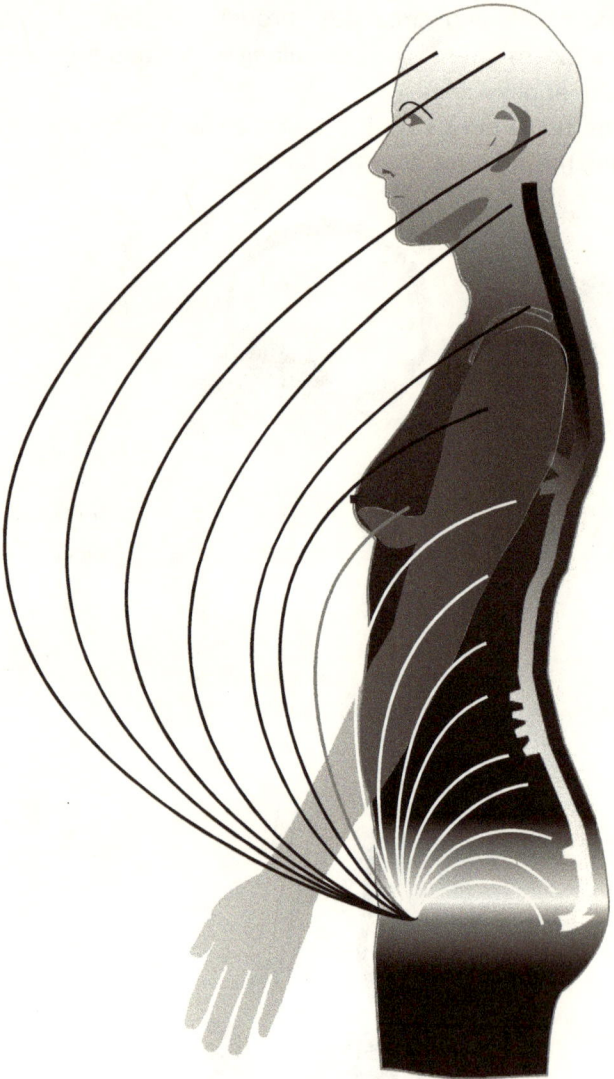

The life force or kundalini cannot radiate in the brain unless the sexual fluids are continually being moved upwards. There might be a surge of spinal energy into the brain but soon after, the energy again settles into the lower spine near the anus and genitals. One can surge the energy by drugs, mantras, breath infusion techniques or by effective visualization; but until one finds a way to move it up continually and permanently, it will be predominant in the lower spine.

There are two types of reproductive fluids produced in the body. One is a heavy type that is carbon dioxided and the other is a light-weight type that is oxygenated. Some persons have a higher percentage of carbon-dioxided blood, which results in a heavier fluid.

This concentrate travels downwards through the genitals. It does not rise to the head unless it is forced upwards by drugs, affirmations, visualization, air infusion or special muscular contractions. Oxygenated blood produces lighter fluids that flow upwards. That light fluid is quite suitable for brain usage in meditation and psychic perception.

Carbonized semen has a lustier charge. It inspires more passion. The oxygenized semen has a cognizing effect. It improves psychic perception.

Diet

Diet is related to sexual performance. It is not unusual for sexual companions to over-eat considerably and to suffer discomfort. Their bellies become distended. At night they engage in a sexual contact since their minds are drawn into the sexual areas by the food pressure on the pubic floor.

sex you!

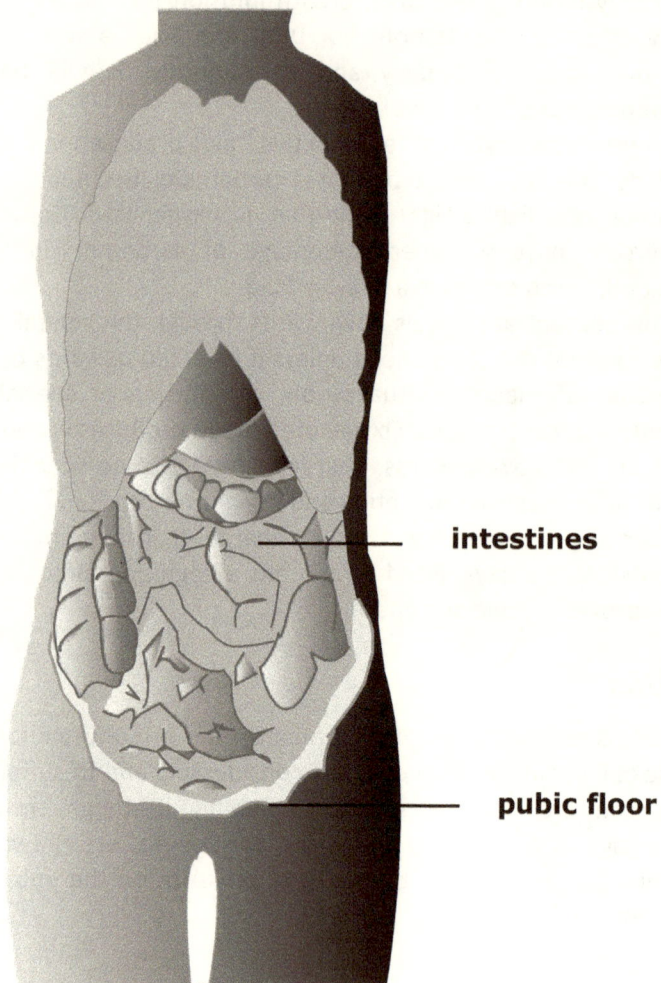

intestines

pubic floor

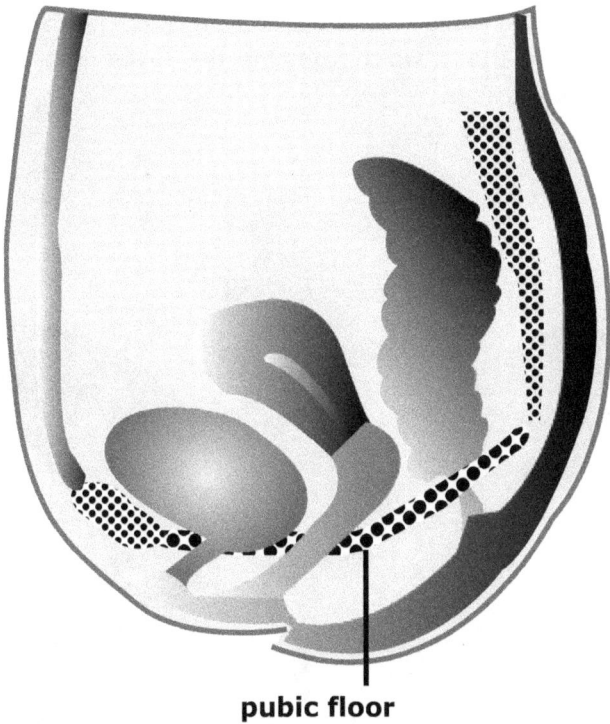

pubic floor

Apart from the quantity of food, there is the spice and protein content. Spices enter the genitals and over-stimulate them to such an extent that one may be forced to have sex contact at the nearest opportunity. High protein and oil-saturated foods, increase sexual secretions. This draws the mind to sex areas of the body, resulting in impulsions. For single people who have no partner, it results in sex dreams and masturbation.

Daily fasting should be practiced until one can do it naturally without effort and without hardship to the body. From a gradual course of daily fasting, the stomach shrinks considerably just as over-eating causes the belly to become distended as if it was designed to protrude

sex you!

outside the body.

Consider the pubic floor of the body. It is the base area of the lower trunk, which contains the lower intestines, genitals and anus.

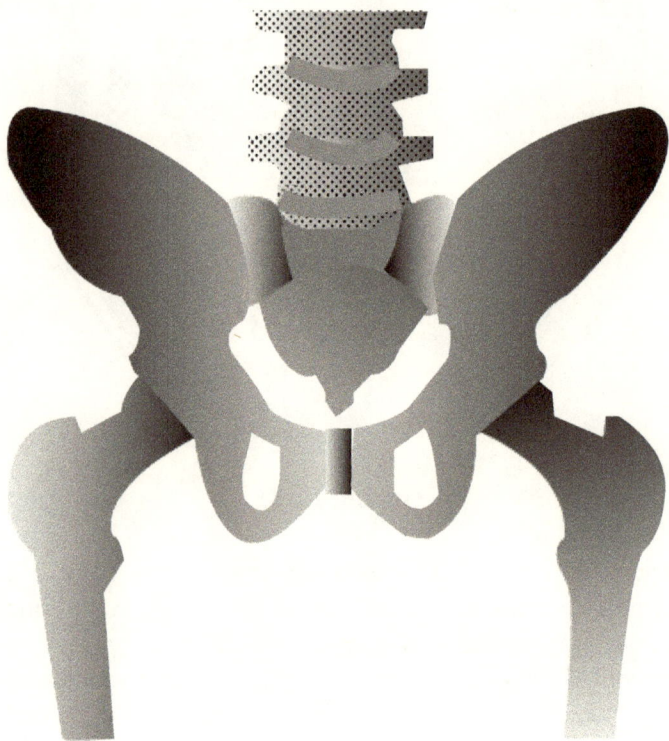

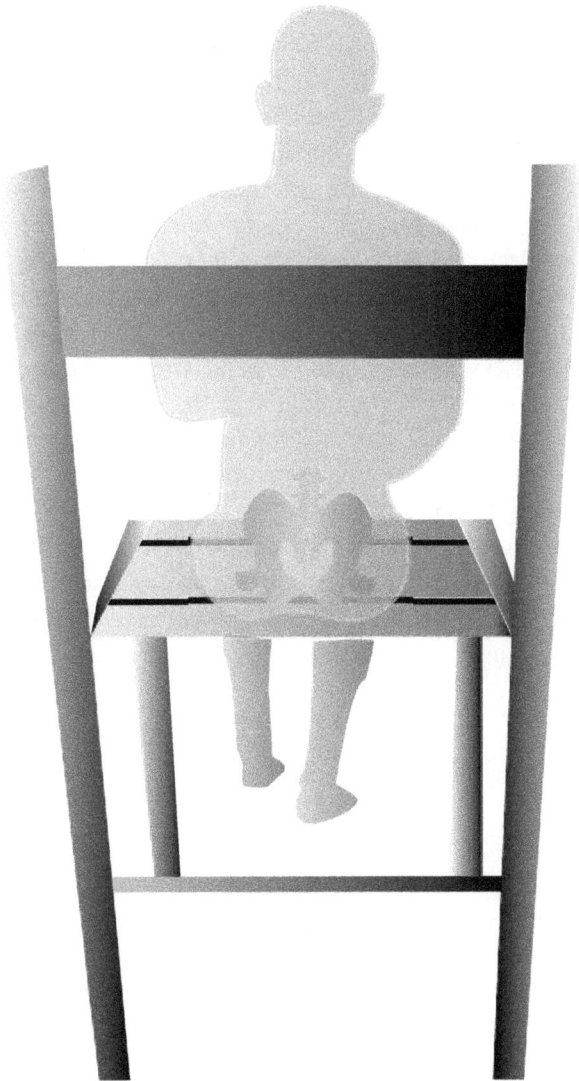

If one eats a main meal in the afternoon or evening, that

food moves through the small intestine during the night. The digestive process requires the muscular movement of the intestinal tubing and the movement of vast quantities of blood during the night. These bodily actions subconsciously remind one of sexual indulgence.

We are concerned here with the muscular activity of the stomach and the small intestines. The large intestines are for the most part, a storage tube. The small intestines have continuous muscular action to squeeze food pulp and extract nutrients. The continuous squeezing and stretching of the small intestines do not cease until all food is processed and emptied into the large intestines. And if this action takes place at night, one's mind is drawn to the lower part of the body, with the result of initiating sex desires. Many persons follow a nightly routine of eating a full meal, passing stool and urine if they are able to, retiring to bed, resting a little while discussing affairs, and then engaging in the gruesome task of sex contact. After sex, they roll over in fatigue and fall asleep. If they are not fully satisfied by the indulgence, they awaken two, three or four hours later and play out the sex again.

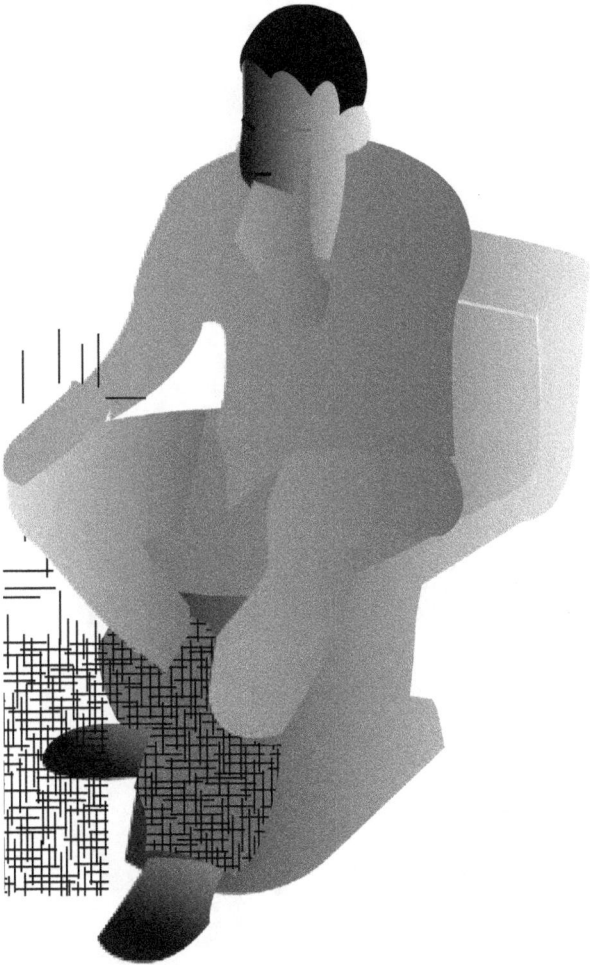

In sex life, satisfaction means thorough fatigue of the organs, where the man's instrument goes limp and his body is drained of semen. His brain becomes dull. His muscles tire. His mind is depressed. After passing semen once, twice or thrice for the most, a man is finished for the session, even if he consumes a high-protein, oil-saturated diet. But if he takes help from liquor, sildenafil citrate, marijuana, valium, cocaine, heroin, LSD, or other aphrodisiacs, he may continue hours of indulgence. Some drugs prolong the intense pleasure. Some keep the male organ erect for hours. Some delay ejaculation.

For a woman it is a bit different. While a man with a sober body is fatigued after passing semen once or twice, a woman's body is not exhausted that easily. As soon as a man discharges semen from a sober body and his organ goes limp, his female partner may become disappointed. Through this many men develop an inferiority complex. To offset that, they take liquor or drugs which prevent the organ from relaxing. In some cases a man passes semen once, twice, or three times and still his female partner

sex you!

does not reach climax. This is because the female body has more sexual stamina.

Unless we can find a method to relieve the pubic floor of food pressure during the night, it will be impossible to decrease the late-night food-sex triggers. Please look at the diagram:

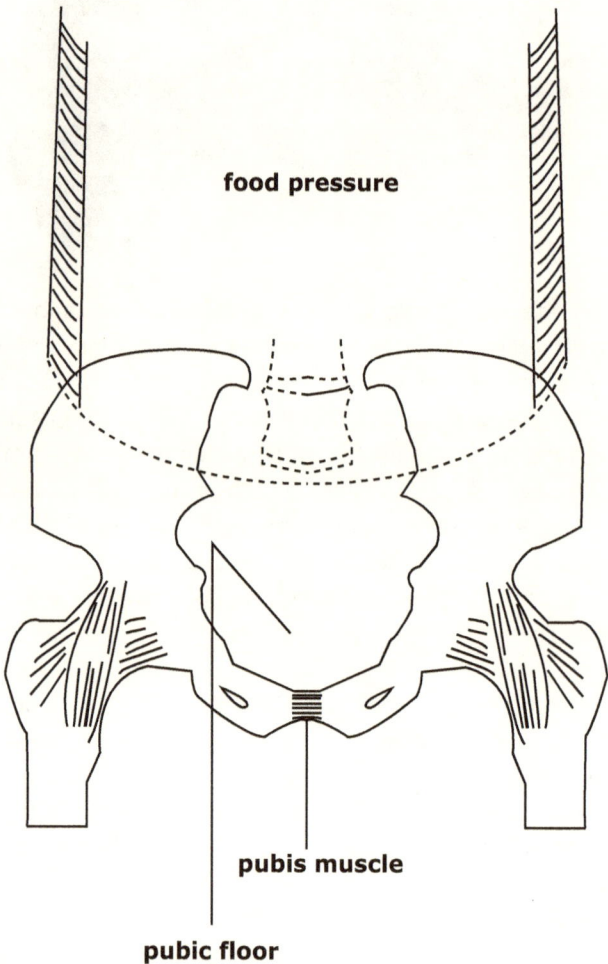

food pressure

pubis muscle

pubic floor

food pressure

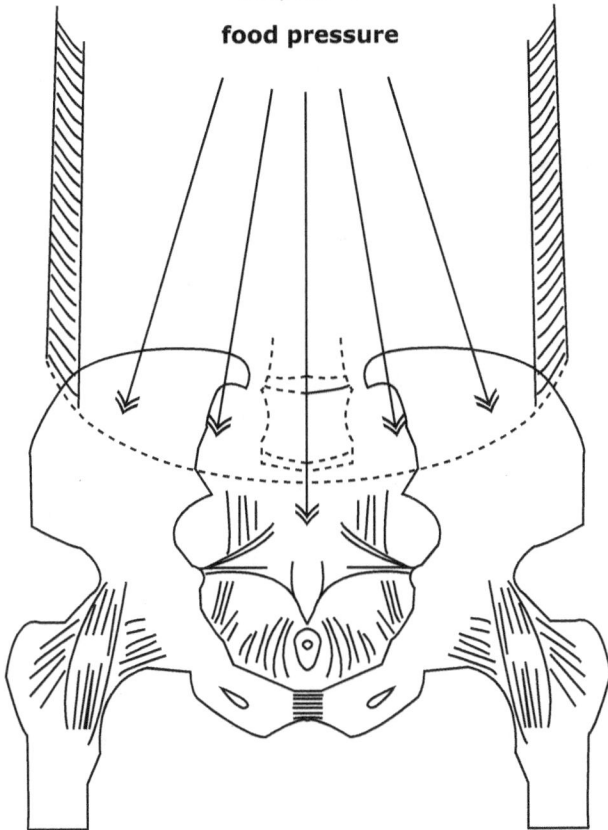

That diagram shows the pubis muscle and the ligament that connects the pubic area to the thigh. This pubis muscle is very important since if it is spread apart under pressure from food in the lower part of the body, it may invoke sexual intercourse. This idea might sound fantastic but let us consider another point to show that this pubis muscle is related to sexual intercourse.

Usually a girl's feet are closer together in her youth and further apart in maturity. And to put it plainly, in the majority of incidences, a female must spread her thighs to engage in sexual intercourse. That is the nature of the act. Furthermore if a young woman develops a pregnancy, her pubis muscle stretches considerably. It stretches the most during parturition when her baby is delivered. In some cases that muscle remains stretched permanently.

In the male body the stretching of that muscle also takes place, but it is hardly noticed since a male body never carries a fetus. However, if a male is sensitive to sex arousal, he may observe that whenever he feels sexually-motivated, his pubis muscle automatically relaxes and energy moves through its ligaments.

If one eats late, the pressure produced in the lower part of the body, will automatically cause the pubis muscle to release sexual energy. The thighs will heat up and one may feel the need for intercourse.

There are muscular contractions which facilitate a reduction in excessive sexual interest. The main one is called sex lock. This contraction consists of pulling the pubic muscles into the body along with the ligaments that connect the inner thighs to the pubic area. There is another lock which pulls the circular anal muscle into the body.

One should adjust the diet to ease the pressure on the pubic floor so that one's attention is not drawn to that area more than necessary. In addition, there should be prompt expulsion of liquid and solid waste. If these remain in the bladder and lower intestines longer than necessary, beyond the first urge to expel them, the mind will wander in these regions and eventually link itself to sexual desire.

Oily foods are nourishing but when eaten in excess the result is passion. Therefore both the type of food and the time eaten, should be regarded.

Sexual indulgence is promoted by food intake, especially by protein intake. When I lived in the tropics in the years of 1986 to 1991, I had no means of income. I did not beg donations but lived on whatever two or three friends would contribute. At the time I supported a wife and four children. Somehow or other, as fated we survived, but it was so bad sometimes that I could not afford a drop of milk for months on end. In any case I made headway in sex restraint. Due to lack of nourishing foods, particularly milk, my teeth shrunk. The enamel declined. I was not fearful however because I sensed a decrease in sexual lust and an increase in psychic focus.

In 1991 under pressure of destiny I returned to the United States. When I did, diet improved. I got milk daily. After about two years, I noticed that most of the enamel that was missing from my teeth re-formed. However, this advantage was accompanied by a disadvantage, because when I took milk steadily I noticed that the sexual secretions in my body increased. The sexual nature again became impulsive. That experience indicated that nourishing foods are supportive of sex desire.

Chapter 4
Sex Procurement

Sexual indulgence is a highlight of mundane pleasures. It is the ultimate basic enjoyment but it entails complete drainage of psychic energy through the genitals. Sexual pleasure is maximum energy utilization. It is exhaustive. In the material world, intimacy or romance means sharing life forces. It does not mean sharing in the intimacy of the soul.

The influence of departed souls who require rebirth should not be overlooked. So much of sex indulgence is forced on by souls who require rebirth. The only avenue through which departed souls can get new physical forms is sex indulgence, either by moral or immoral contact. To the dearly departed, sexual contact is everything in terms of returning to this world. And to us, after we leave the present bodies and require rebirth here, sexual contact will be the only avenue. To the ancestors who are not liberated to higher worlds, sexual relationship is vital. It is their priority. They would do anything to encourage it.

Generally speaking, those who are departed find parents that suit their status and tendency. Usually, a commoner cannot take birth from wealthy parents but a deceased person who had wealth, might take birth from poverty-stricken parents.

An ancestor first enters the feelings and then the blood stream. It flows to the genitals and remains lodged there until there is an opportunity for rebirth or until it is relocated and moves into another parental body.

Situationally, the soul can be so tiny, so miniscule, so microscopic that it can take possession of something as tiny as a virus or an idea. A sexual thought in one's mind might not be a thought but a soul force, a spiritual entity. If one does not realize this one might identify fully with the fantasy. If one can instantly realize that an idea is possessed by an entity requiring rebirth or that it is transmitted by such an entity, one can sidestep the sexual fantasy or urge and remain steady.

The organs have a life of their own. The female genitalia is a type of mouth which relishes the male sexual organ and extracts juices from it. While we enjoy the openings, our sense of enjoyment and our emotional registry is superimposed and confused with the organ's consumption capacity.

After years of struggling in this present body to overcome impulsive sexual behavior, I reached a stage where I could review impulsive behavior as an aggregate energy from which I was freed. The hugs, kisses, passes of romantic lust, flows of lusty energies in mind and body, in addition to flirtations, minor or major, and all sexual victimizations, were all caused by psychic power. This energy was not controlled by me. While I was involved I could not sort my participation but now, from a distance, the components can be seen. Before I was bewildered and thought it was a mixture of my power and that of others. Now I see with clarity that a minute portion of my power was involved. I was mixed in with other forces and could not realize how I was used in the indulgences because I was overpowered by the enjoying energy.

When a couple first gets married, embraces are spontaneous because of the strong attraction of their life forces. However, once children are generated, a couple can gradually reduce sexual participation and replace it with shared services in other ways, especially spiritual cultivation and mandatory services for cultural refinement.

In a lusty body the life force looks through the senses for sexual opportunities at every moment. It promotes flirtatious encounters. Until it is diverted this never stops.

sex you!

An old man who is impotent, may still retain a lusty interest which remains intact in his subtle form. As soon as he gets a new body in the next life, he will pursue sex again. Old age does not remove sex desire but rather puts it into dormancy. Many elderly men eyeball young girls and enjoy what they see visually even though they cannot engage physically. Some engage in dreams through the subtle body. Some elderly women enjoy the limbs and sexual contours of young male bodies.

One might feel that one should go near someone to converse with the person but the actual reason may be the need of the life force to find its favorite enjoyment which is lusty energy. While one is convinced that the association is lust-free, the life force may enjoy a sexual contact through the eyes and ears and eventually one will be sexually engaged. If one is perceptive of the subtle body, one will be aware of having dreams of sexual contact with the persons to whom one is attracted for other purposes. Those who are not conscious of dreams have no chance for realizing this.

sex you!

Indulgence

The indulgence force that operates the sexual impulse supports itself three ways:

- **by suppressing critical analysis**
- **by providing happiness**
- **by inspiring justifications for its operations**

The indulgence force absorbs the attention of the soul to such an extent that it causes a total loss of objectivity and produces stupor in consciousness. It is like an awful and deep darkness that gradually and steadily overcomes the brilliance of a flame. The purpose of brilliance is to illuminate but if the darkness is deep and dense, the brilliance is frustrated.

The dulling force is represented in the bloodstream as carbonized, stagnant, slowly-circulated blood which flows through the veins in the torso, thighs, legs and feet of the body. This power is fully supportive of frequent indulgence and of sluggish excretory habits through which the body becomes chronically constipated. This dulling power saturates the mind with procrastination and stupor. The dulling power pulls the life force, the emotions and reasoning faculties into the lower portions of the body. A person who is chronically constipated is attentive to the bowels, the anal sphincter muscle and the buttocks area. Due to the constipated condition, the person's consciousness remains concerned there. A person who is preoccupied with sex indulgence is focused in the sex organs. During sexual indulgence and especially during sexual climax, one's mind, consciousness, feelings and thinking power, practically everything that is psychological about oneself, is drawn into the sexual area.

Passion is the prime energy for sex drive. It provides most of the encouragement for flirtations. While the dulling power completely absorbs consciousness and provides no feedback, the passionate energies use consciousness and provide positive and negative feedback.

Indulgence also involves a certain amount of reason or justification for the activity. Especially in human societies where there are enforced moral values, the indulgent powers utilize reasoning to create justifications for disapproved sexual acts.

The passionate force first provides enthusiasm but later it creates avenues for the depressing influence. One becomes sleepy and sluggish after climax. One's intellect becomes perceptively stunted because of the lack of oxygenated blood in the gross body and lack of fresh psychic energy in the subtle one.

Chapter 5
Subtle Body Habits

The subtle body is a challenge. That body is even more indulgent than the gross one. In the hereafter, those entities who require rebirth in gross bodies rush here and there in a mad craze to find sexual intercourse which is their gateway to this world. In some heavenly places, angelic beings engage in intercourse without risk of producing children.

As soon as one achieves physical restraint, the subtle body increases psychic sexual activities. Thus many who have no physical participation, may experience wet dreams.

If the gross body is impulsive, then the subtle one is a greater challenge since it has the ability to move from one sex partner to another in a jiffy without respect to time or place. The subtle body does not have to catch a plane or bus to go to another city. It can travel as rapidly as thought, moving from one astral location to another instantly. Its unrestrained motion effectively contravenes restraint.

First, one curbs the gross body and lastly one restrains the subtle one. The subtle form lags in control. In fact when the gross one is completely curbed, the subtle one increases its sexual pursuits.

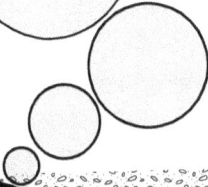

There is a story in the legends of the *Mahābhārata*, where a warrior named Arjuna mastered sexual expression through yoga disciplines. He then developed the psychic side and was transported to heaven. When he arrived he was shocked to observe how sexually-permissive many angelic beings were. His aunt, a celestial woman named Urvashee, met him as soon as he settled in. She offered herself sexually. He refused. Feeling rejected, she cursed him with one year of impotence in his earthly body. As a result he did in fact function as a eunuch, named Brihan, when he returned to the earth and lived in the territory of King Virat. Sex impulse is predominant in some heavenly worlds.

In a gross form on an earthly planet we are sheltered from the sexual ravishes of heavenly life but no such protection will be rendered after we separate from this gross world at the death of the present physical body.

The subtle body has little or no objectivity. It is involved in unrestricted enjoyment, being concerned with sensual life in the form of eating gourmet edibles in heavenly places, dancing, wearing of sheer clothing, smelling nice fragrances and most of all engaging in acrobatic sexual intercourses.

sex you!

Some earthly people try to reach these heavenly places by taking drugs like LSD, opium and cocaine. Thus they enjoy unrestricted happiness in the subtle body while they still have gross forms. Drugs might afford the user hours of sexual pleasure, where the gross and subtle bodies secrete sexual fluids profusely until the drug wears off.

Psychic perception

Sexual restraint can cause an increase in psychic perception and dream recall. It may increase conscious hours and decrease sleeping time. It makes rest more efficient. One can become more conscious in the astral world on a nightly basis when the subtle body disengages from the gross one. This disengagement is required for the health of the gross form since during the disengagement the physical body is rested. Usually, people go into sleeping stupor when the subtle form disengages but with sexual restraint even to a slight degree, subtle perception may increase.

When the sexual energy reaches the brain, it is said that the life force is elevated. At that time the sexual fluids circulate evenly throughout the body and do not accumulate in the genitals. The blood circulation in the gross body increases and the solarized subtle air circulates more freely in the subtle form, making that form appear bright and clear. Since sexual hormones are no longer stored in the lower torso of the body, the life force no longer stays there because it is attracted to sex hormones. It moves up the spine into the brain. The usual stupor and ignorance go away. The person becomes more brilliant and more perceptive of spiritual reality.

sex you!

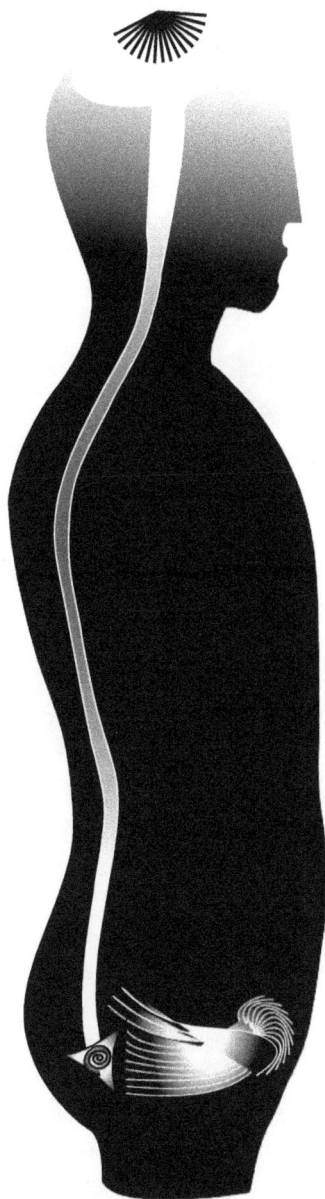

As nature would have it, one gets a partner and links sexually. Then one enters the stupor of fatigue and sleep. In heterosexual situations, when the man is exhausted, the woman may not be. In the case of a man, his body is built in such a way that the orgasm of pleasure occurs much quicker than that of a female. A woman is likely to keep waiting and waiting in expectation of the desired climax. As a result a man may be required to sex himself to exhaustion if he has to please such a woman.

We get some information about this in the legend of Kardama and Devahuti. Kardama, a proficient yogi, split himself into nine versions and sexed his wife in nine different variations to her satisfaction. Her body required nine times the satisfaction required for his.

In the beginning cohabitation means sexing and then entering a stupor, then sleeping like logs, then crawling out of bed in the morning to meet daylight. This is the history of sexual partnership.

Value of semen

Yogi Bhajan once said that one drop of semen is worth at least eighty drops of blood. Semen is that vital. Higher yoga rests on the foundation of conservation of semen from sexual interest. Higher consciousness is dependent on semen reaching the brain to activate the brow and crown chakras.

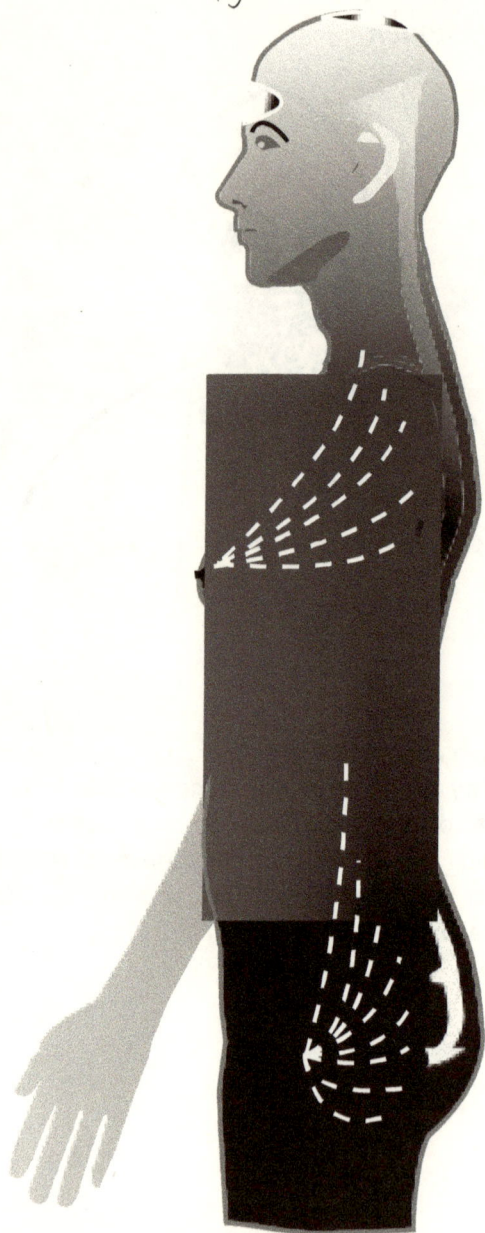

We may contest the accuracy of the ratio of one to eighty *(1:80)* but it is a biological fact that much blood is strained in the testes to manufacture a drop of semen. When a male body ejaculates semen, it becomes exhausted. It requires rest to restore vitality. It is also a fact that occasionally women become irritable during the menstrual cycle when they lose ova and other fluids.

The two prominent chakras in the brain are the brow and crown chakras. The brow center concerns visual perception. The crown concerns elevation of feeling or consciousness. As far as the crown chakra is concerned, there is no chance of awakening it or perceiving it if one wastes semen. It is simply impossible since wastage of semen causes low semen flow in the brain which results in dullness in the crown chakra. One can, however, awaken the brow chakra even if one depletes semen.

There is an exception, whereby one can open the brow or crown chakras with narcotic or psycho-active drugs like heroin or lysergic acid *(LSD)*. However these methods are counterproductive. When the chakras are opened by drugs, they close down tighter after the effect of the drug wears off. The increased psychic perception received through these substances disappears after the drug wears off. Then the chakras close down tighter and the life force retreats further into its grotto in the lower spine. In addition, a drug experience, though real, has to be interpreted correctly before it can produce any fruitful result. Many drug users become happy-go-lucky, non-productive, simple-minded human beings.

Drugs are a cheap form of elevation which may be followed by a hellish mental depression. Regular usage of drugs may cause adaptation to an animal embryo in the next birth.

sex you!

Perception of the spiritual dimensions beyond the astral worlds, is only possible if one develops the crown chakra. If one develops the brow chakra, one can see the souls who hover in the astral world waiting for rebirth. One can get glimpses of the angelic people who live permanently in the celestial world.

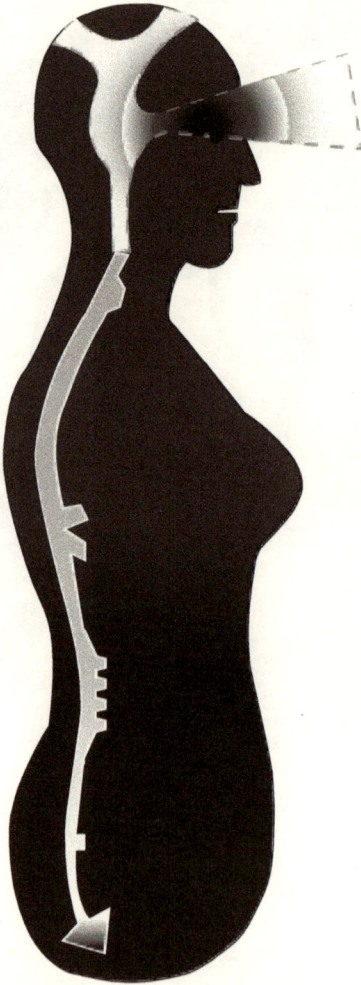

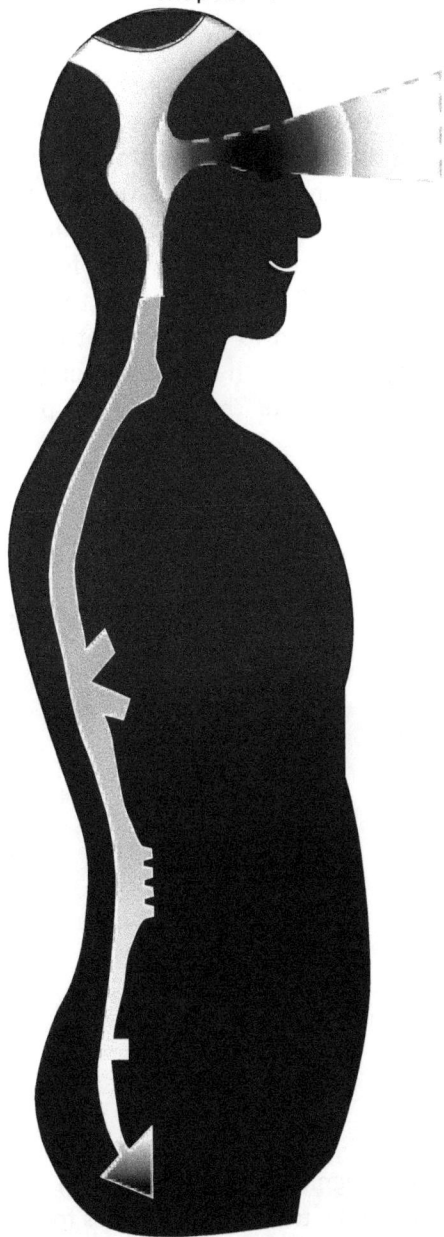

The movement of semen

Semen is rarely distributed throughout the body. In fact, due to slow circulation in the torso, groin and thighs, semen stays in the lower areas most of the time, awaiting discharge through the genitals. In the climax of sexual pleasure, semen is emitted and simultaneously every cell of the body contributes some energy for the flow of plasma to the testes. This energy goes to the testes for the creation of more semen to replace what is emitted in a sexual discharge. In the flush of sexual energy, all the cells of the body get involved. This is why the pleasure is so intense.

There is such a significant contribution of energy from each cell of the body, that usually a child's form resembles the parents. This is called genetic influence but it is based on the contribution of every cell in the body for the manufacture of semen in the testes and ova in the ovaries. The quality of the semen determines the high-class or low-class body created. A high-class body has cultured tendencies while a low-class one exhibits vices and perverted habits. Any type of human body can be reformed but it is better to begin life with a high-tendency body.

The life force is possessed of immature living entities who will, after billions of years, become evolved enough to get their own advanced forms. They are being given some orientation to creature life by their habitation of life force. Thus everyone who has an animal body has such a life force with a host of immature entities being composite parts of it. Because these entities have yet to develop an exterior sense of perception, they are survival-crazy in terms of trying to control the senses; directing the nose to smell, the mouth to speak and taste, the eyes to see, the skin to feel and the ears to hear. They act impulsively because they are below an edge, having nothing but a membrane for an outer sensing mechanism. Thus every predominant thinker in every created body is not the only thinker in the body, but he or she is the most prominent of limited selves who inhabit the form. The work for salvation or tendency towards further implication quickens or retards the progress of the immature entities who live in the psyche.

sex you!

Chapter 6
Haphazard Rebirth

When there is a gender mismatch between the psyche and physical body, that is experienced as an incongruence between the psychological and physical profiles of the person. There are two main causes of gender mismatch, namely, haphazard transmigration of the soul from one body to another, and crossing into different species of life without divine insight.

In the process of transmigration, one absorbs diverse influences. When one gets a human body one carries into it, tendencies from former lives. Unless restricted, one reestablishes previous habits.

If we could see someone's conduct in a series of past lives and if we could see what that person was subjected to in the interim state after leaving the previous body and developing a new one, we would not be amazed at anyone's expressions. Our amazement is due to lack of insight into former lives. Due to lack of recall, most people who accept the view of reincarnation do not accept it deeply enough to act on it in their daily lives. They are confined to information about the current life, with no access to what happened before.

According to Krishna in the *Bhagavad Gītā*, the individual spirit leaves one body and goes to the hereafter. If it did not assume a higher profile before death of its body, it develops as an embryo in this world sooner or later.

Krishna explained that the soul carries different profiles from one body to another just as the air transports aromas. As facilitated by providence, the soul obtains a body which has a certain type of nose, tongue, eye, membrane and ear. These are configured in the mind.

According to the body received, the soul is restricted to a particular set of commodities.

There is a connection between moving from one body to another and picking up non-reproductive sexual habits. As long as we forget previous behaviors, we are prone to uninformed activities. We lose track of identity and mistake body tendency for personality. Even a well-behaved person can, in the next life, display the same irregular behavior he or she criticized in others previously. It would depend on the type of parentage one receives. Since one will not remember the past, one may identify with irregular behaviors in any future life.

Crossing into different species

Crossing from one body to another in the same species is one type of complication. Even that requires much psychological adjustments. Usually, one forgets the past experience and denies the past life as soon as one becomes self conscious in a new body. Thus transmigration even in the same species is bewildering.

Crossing from one species to another is even more complicated. Only a great soul who is reserved in spiritual focus and who is naturally detached from the senses, can do so safely without losing the human perspective. Usually one who falls from the human species goes down further unless some divine grace is bestowed upon the person. In one legend about life in the celestial world, a king named Indra once came to ruination and was profiled to take a hog body. In the process of animal life he forgot the royal status. Usually a person who goes down to the animal world becomes preoccupied with beastly tendencies and forgets the higher profiles.

Arjuna, the hero of the *Bhagavad Gītā*, once rescued five angelic girls who assumed reptilian forms and were transmigrating in the crocodile species for some time. The compassionate Arjuna killed the crocodile bodies. By his influence, the angels resumed angelic existence and abandoned the reptilian identity.

However, there are individuals who are moving up into the human species, just as others are moving down into the animal kingdom. In the upward movement, the souls carry lower habits from previous species and awkwardly adjust to the standard of responsibility approved for humans.

There is a danger of irresponsible sexual expression even for those who took successive human forms for many lives. The human body is animalistic to a degree. It takes a deliberate effort for a human being to resist vulgarities and thus suppress animal nature. It is only training in skills and morals, as well as cultural restraints, which suppresses the animal urges within the human psyche. We are handicapped by the inability to transcend past conditionings, even those of this life, what to speak of habits and tendencies which are present in the subconscious from previous material bodies.

Chapter 7
Gender Complications

A disembodied entity who craves physical existence would do any and everything to force a human being to indulge in sexual intercourse, even if such intercourse does not give an embryo. People in the ghostly or astral realms who require rebirth and who cannot find willing parents to beget their infant forms, are under certain pressure. They are in great anxiety, in desperation of manifesting a body on earth. As such they are not particularly fond of sexual restrictions.

A disembodied entity, who enters into the body of a human being of either sex, will not be particularly careful to observe if that person is male or female. The disembodied entity detects the lusty energy, not the polarity of it. Even though they desire the result of a human body they might enter into the lusty nature of a homosexual, induce and encourage sex in his mind and emotions, be emitted from his body in a semen discharge in the anus of another male, or in masturbation, only to find out that no embryo develops as a result.

Some disembodied entitles who are subjected to a mini-death by being emitted as semen into anuses and through masturbation, were homosexuals in the past life or encouraged the habit. They are subjected to frustration when their liquid sperm forms repeatedly die in non-reproductive intercourses.

Controlling deities

The sex organs have need for sexual indulgence. Unless these organs are allowed the minimum sexual fluids or hormones, there is no question of controlling them. The organs themselves are tasting instruments of the body, just as the tongue is such an organ, except that the sexual organs taste feelings. Sexual pleasure is more or less the taste of the disembodied souls' eagerness for life and their lust for physical bodies.

Each sex organ has a controlling deity who regulates its usage. This deity is a supernatural personality. In its highest aspect, the organ is reproductively-inclined, and influences for responsible family life. In that state a particular deity controls it. In its median aspect, it is lusty, passionate, and supportive of casual sex and irresponsibility. In that condition, it is controlled by another supernatural personality. In its diseased, afflicted or masochistic condition, another mystic existence takes possession of it. The organ is demanding, but it is the controlling deity that has the need and not the organ itself. When the deity craves overindulgence, the organ becomes ravenous for it.

The sexual organ tastes for the controlling deity, to the extent that the female organ functions as fleshy jaws which eat pleasurable feelings. The male organ functions as a moving, licking tongue for the same. In the case of the female organ, it tries to chew and eat the fleshy male organ and in so doing it enjoys varieties of sexual pleasure. All the same, the male organ tastes the fleshy cylindrical female part as if a tongue relishes pieces of stewed meat.

No other impulse is able to drain away our energy and attention as much as sexual pleasure. It is the most powerful mundane experience. It is a most powerful vice, making it a big challenge for those who desire abstinence.

Sexual design

Many humans have a keen interest regarding the pleasure experienced by women during intercourse. Much media is available illustrating how women can have intense pleasure with discharge of fluids. A woman may manipulate the organ to experience an orgasm, which may occur easily or after prolonged fondling.

For men ejaculation comes quickly since nature designed a male body to emit semen and not to hold embryos in pregnancies. The male orgasm is part of the ejaculation procedure for transmitting sperm into the body of a woman.

The pleasure men feel when discharging semen is interpreted in many ways. That enjoyment is an electrified potency through which disembodied souls are rushed out of a man's body, for the formulation of embryos.

The female body is not designed to produce semen. It produces ova, which accommodates semen, but the female system has a clitoris which medical experts attest to be a reduction of a potential male organ. This means that initially, each embryo is capable of either sex. It begins as neuter and either changes into a male or develops as female.

With an indentation in the pubic area initially, the human embryos all appear somewhat female. Those which evolve male gender, have that slit knitted together. Evidence of this is present in the form of the scar line which traverses the bottom of the male testes.

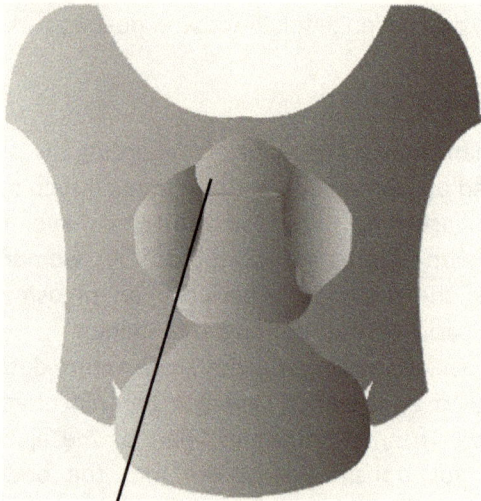

rudimentary sex organs of both genders

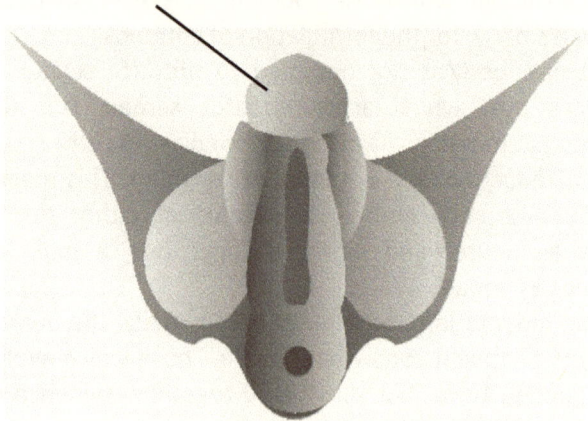

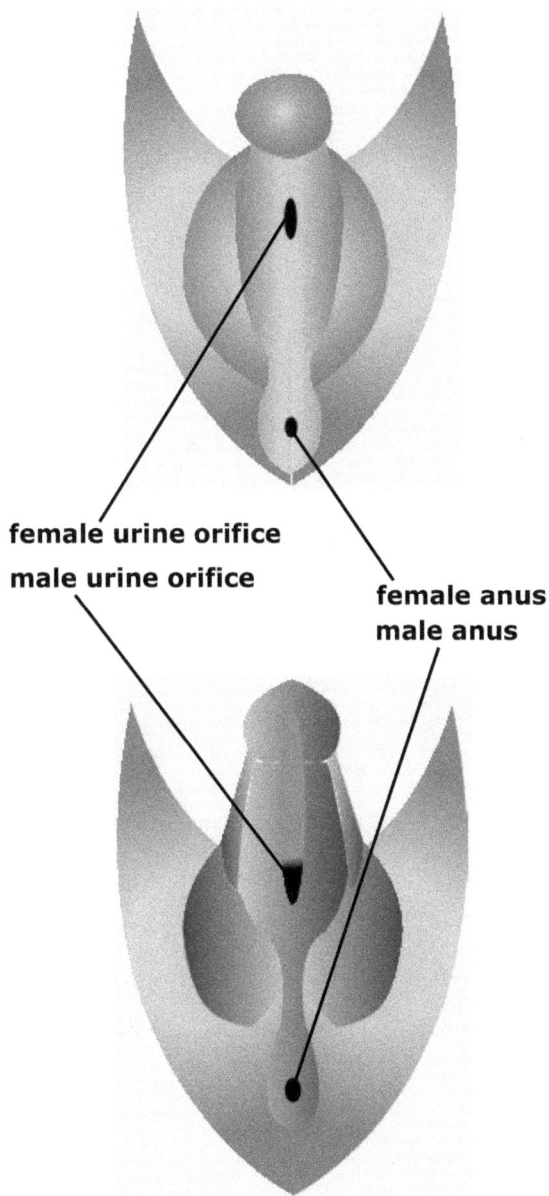

female urine orifice
male urine orifice

female anus
male anus

sex you!

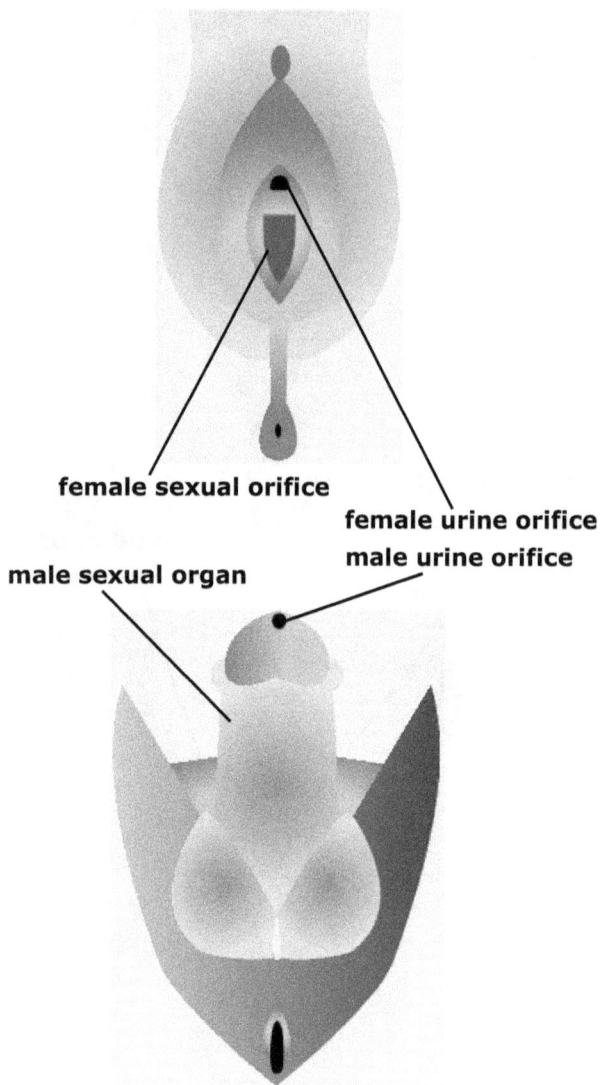

female sexual orifice

female urine orifice
male urine orifice

male sexual organ

Transsexuals

There is an interesting legend in the *Mahābhārata*, about Princess Shikhand who was transsexual. She was born a female body, but her father, King Drupad, preferred a son. The deity Shiva promised the father that the infant would change into a male in the near future. This did not happen immediately. Still the King proclaimed that the baby was masculine. However, when Shikhand reached sexual maturity and her body began to menstruate, King Drupad tried to find a wife for her since he was confident that before the wedding ceremony, the girl's gender would be changed miraculously. He considered that Shiva's word would materialize if Shikhand was duly married.

Drupad arranged to marry his so-called son, who was in fact his daughter, to a princess who was from another country. The bride's father was a powerful king named Hiranyavarna. The marriage was royal and grand. During the honeymoon, the bride discovered that she was duped into marrying a female. She alerted her maids. They informed her father, King Hiranyavarna. He became angry. This king then threatened to kill King Drupad and Princess Shikhand. He sent a message telling Drupad to prepare for battle. He mobilized his army, took help from allies, and proceeded in battle array to Drupad's city.

In the meantime, King Drupad discussed the matter with his ministers, who were told that Shikhand was indeed a female, though her sex was to change by the promise of a deity. Nevertheless King Drupad began fortifying his city since he knew for a fact that his brother-in-law, King Hiranyavarna, was enroute for war.

For her part, Princess Shikhand began to regret the incidence. She considered that the danger could be averted if she were to leave the city to reach the deity or commit suicide. It so happened that she entered an enchanted place which was owned by a supernatural being. In that place, a magician named Stuna, lived in a white-plastered brick mansion. He sensed the presence of Shikhand and was informed of her whereabouts. They met by his arrangement. Shikhand explained the difficulty her father encountered on her behalf.

Stuna was a capable mystic. He was empowered to give favors for the fulfillment of desires. He said, "I can help if you are in difficulty. I am Stuna, the sky ranger. I do sorcery."

Shikhand replied, "The only way to appease the conquering Hiranyavarna is to change my sex into that of a man. If I can manifest masculinity, he would desist as he would be assured that his daughter could bear a child for me."

Without hesitation, Stuna said, "So be it. Use my sexual organ and vigor and I will assume your privacy and modesty. There is one condition. You must return here within a reasonable period of time so that I can resume my gender."

Shikhand was relieved. She said, "I will come back as soon as my assumed masculinity is verified to the satisfaction of my father-in-law, and as soon as his warriors are withdrawn from our city."

By mystic power, Stuna reversed the gender. Shikhand became a man. Stuna took her femininity in turn. As a male Princess Shikhand returned home. He informed his father. The King was relieved. He sent news to Hiranyavarna, saying, "You are excited over nothing, my dear brother-in-law. You mobilized an army over a false alarm. Come! Inspect, if you think that my son is not a man."

After getting that message, King Hiranyavarna, that proud conquering man, sent some experienced young women to check the sex of Shikhand. When they reported that he had a male organ, the King was pleased. He met Drupad in an agreeable mood. They dined and associated together.

In the meantime, Stuna met with difficulty. His authority, a supernatural being named Kubera, came to the mansion. Kubera expected a grand welcome since he was accustomed to receiving honors and greetings everywhere he went. When his flying conveyance hovered over the mansion of Stuna, he heard no festivities. He got no response. He told his assistant, "Go at once and drag that arrogant and lazy Stuna. He knows I am here. He understands my taste. Still he remains cooped up in the mansion."

The servant went to see Stuna. He returned to Kubera and said, "Your servant Stuna is now a woman. He knowingly exchanged his gender for the femininity of Shikhand who, though born a girl, was declared as a boy by her parents initially. Stuna met Princess Shikhand, who was dis-heartened because her father was placed under siege. To help the Princess, he used magical powers to exchange her sex with his. He is ashamed to greet you as that female body."

Hearing this, Kubera, the supernatural person, became annoyed. He exclaimed, "This foolish servant of mine acted whimsically. Since he never consulted me, let him be a woman indefinitely."

Hearing of the curse, Stuna, who traded masculinity for a feminine body, begged Kubera for pardon. Kubera said, "In that case, accept the femininity for the life span of Shikhand. When she is killed in battle, you may resume your identity."

In this story Stuna became compassionate towards Shikhand. Subsequently, the supernatural being Kubera became annoyed. Stuna had to accept the sex change for many years, even though initially it was intended to be for a few months only. This story was told by Bhishma to Duryodhan in the *Mahābhārata*.

Psychology from previous lives

Once we accept transmigration as a fact, we need to review the dynamics of the process. Information is given in books like *Bhagavad Gītā*. Transmigration occurs on the basis of the subtle body. If that body becomes vulgar, the earthly body formed on the basis of it, will be prone to similar habits. If the subtle body is reformed, one will either go to the celestial regions, be liberated, or take a vice-resistant human form.

The effect of the subtle body on the hereafter is described by Krishna in the *Bhagavad Gītā*:

> *Moreover, whatever texture of existence is recalled when a person abandons his body in the end, to that same type of life, he is projected, O son of Kuntī, always being transformed into that status of life. (8.6)*

The next body is based on the tendencies that are assumed in this life. One may have a human form now but if one cultivates vulgarity, one will be familiar with that at the time of death, and the subtle body will assume a corresponding profile.

Krishna explained:

> *Regardless of whichever body that master acquires, or whichever one he departs from, he goes taking these senses along, just as the wind goes with the perfumes from their source.(Bhagavad Gītā 15.8)*

If the gross body has certain diseases or perverse tendencies, the next physical body may also have such defects, regardless of whether such a body is human or animal. Some people are so afraid of going down to a lower species of life that they flatly deny the possibility, but unfortunately a denial is no guarantee. Positive thinking alone will not prevent what is undesirable, even though it does save us from worrying about negative possibilities.

Presently there is much literature for and against homosexual behavior, but it will suffice to say that the medical profession is becoming more and more accepting of it. Authoritative medical data is printed, which states that homosexuality is acceptable, natural and good. Masturbation is appraised as well.

Many psychologists research the causes of homosexual behavior. Many accept masturbation, homosexuality and lesbian relations as natural; but they pry into a person's background to see if such tendencies were genetic or associative.

Unless one pries into previous life-times, one cannot really understand the cause of a behavior. The approach of the psychologists is better than the efforts of the religious fanatics and medical professionals, but still it is insufficient. Psychological factors from one's childhood are important but such analysis is incomplete without information about previous lives.

Chapter 8
Gender Complication
Details

If, for instance, one has a male body and one feels that one should play the part of a female, and if to one's mind one preferred to be born a woman, it may mean that one was a woman in a previous life. One's subtle body may be a female psychology. Thus, it feels uncomfortable in a male physical form. Admittedly there is no memory of the previous life but the female tendency is proof of those traits in the subtle body.

On occasion, there are variations to this. For instance, a boy who was very close to his mother, might easily absorb feminine tendencies in her association. After that exposure he might feel compelled to exhibit a feminine mentality. He might find the male form to be awkward and foreign. The mere idea that when we take a new body in a different lineage, we strongly identify with that family, signifies that our instinct is to attach ourselves indiscriminately to a birth environment. On that basis, it is quite possible for a boy to assume feminine nature or for a girl to acquire the masculine mentality.

There is the legend of King Sudyu. He was the son of Manu. When Sudyu took birth he emerged in a feminine body. There was a glitch in the genetic structure of the body. It was produced on the basis of his mother's desire for a daughter. In that case a mother's wish prevailed to cause a feminine body for someone with a masculine identity. After Sudyu's birth as a female infant, the father, Manu, who was disappointed, consulted with the mystic priest who conducted the conception ceremony. The priest explained that a junior priest was influenced by the Queen to visualize a girl's profile in the rituals. The senior priest petitioned a deity and the sex of the child was reversed, causing a male sex organ and male traits to replace the female ones.

Later, King Sudyu rode on horseback into the forest with some government officials. As he rode he journeyed deep into a forest and entered an enchanted territory. Upon entering that magical place, his sex was altered into that of a woman and so were the bodies of his ministers and their stallions.

King Sudyu was born as a girl child named Ila. His infant female body was changed into a male one by Vasisht, the mystic priest. Then as an adult male, it reverted into a beautiful, sexually-appealing adult female. When Sudyu noticed the sexual transformation, he was surprised to find himself in that predicament. However, neither he nor any of his ministers assumed a lesbian profile, but the King, who was now a queen to his dismay, fell in love with a man named Budha and had a child for that man.

Later by a favor from the mystic priest, Sudyu became a transgender, alternating monthly by changing into the opposite gender. He was Queen Ila for a month; King Sudyu for the following month. That is how he lived for many years.

In another legend, a certain King Puran was very attached to his wife. As a result of cultivating this attachment he thought of a woman's psychology at the time of death. In the next life he took a feminine form and became the wife of a man. In one life he was the husband of a wife and in the succeeding life he was the wife of a husband. This is what is meant when Krishna said that one assumes a body according to one's demeanor at the time of death. Puran did not willfully plan to take any other earthly body for that matter. He was like an ordinary human being who has faith in one body only. He passed on however. Since he was preoccupied with female genitalia, he took a female body in the next life.

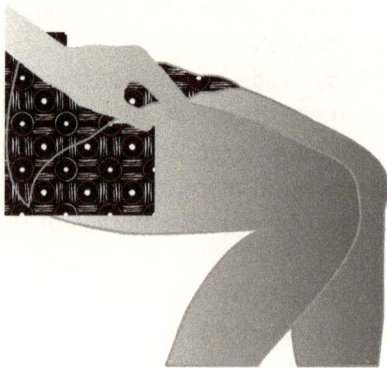

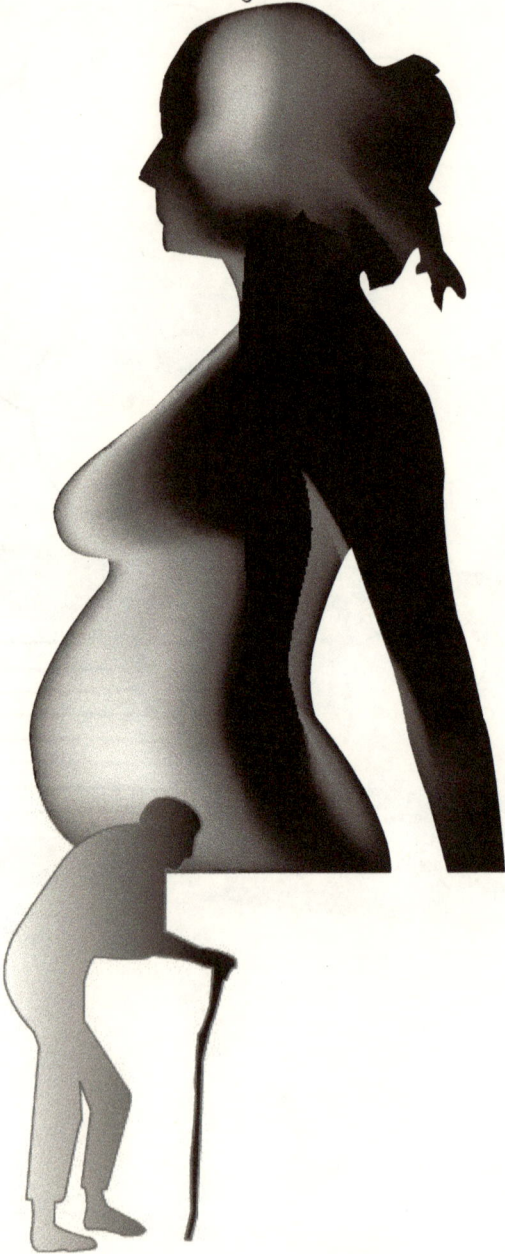

Apart from the psychological sexual variations created in the mind, emotions, perceptions and intentions, there are social conditions which may cause one to adopt particular sexual habits. We are susceptible to outward influences regardless of whether these influences penetrate deep into our psychic nature or not. We are easily adjusted by social pressures from the external world. In fact sexual behavior has much to do with the social pressure applied to us by peers and media.

In the animal kingdom many male animals are insensitive to the responsibility for a mate and offspring. They simply indulge during a certain season and then drift off and leave the raising of progeny to the female who is taxed with pregnancy. In the modern era we find that many women avoid domestic services. Some go to gyms and work out by lifting weights. They develop muscular bodies.

Some take male hormone treatments which change their sexual mood, making them aggressive. Many adopt lesbian activities as the husband or wife of another woman.

Some female animals herd together and do not rely on males since most males show sexual interest without the least concern for progeny. Many females in lower species stick together in groups and range here and there, fending for themselves and their young. When these entities enter the human species they continue the habit of social cooperation.

A male entity who transmigrated from a lower species of life, would be resistant to the paternal responsibility if he was not inclined to it in other species. Similarly, women who came from such species would be disinclined from relying on males. They would easily reject males or have little or no confidence in them. Women of this nature prefer to sororitize with other females.

Homosexuality among males exists in the animal kingdom. Some tendencies in human males may be residual habits from animal births, where a stallion might ride another stallion or a billy-goat might mount another male of its own species.

Chapter 9
Gay/Lesbian Lifestyle

The dominant lesbian

The woman who plays the domineering or prominent decision-making role in a lesbian relationship should consider that if she develops a physical and psychological male profile, she is indirectly initiating a male body in the next life. If that is not what she desires, she should decrease the male outlook and identify more as a female. If she is determined to be male, she should put her thinking and imaginary energies into the idea of getting a male body in the next life.

A lesbian who plays the male role should think, "I wanted to be a man but somehow or the other I developed a female form. If I am patient and bear on with this body until its death, I will certainly evolve the form preferred."

There is a related story in the Vedic history concerning the past life of the same Princess Shikhand who was mentioned before. In the immediate past life she was a woman named Princess Amba. She was kidnapped by General Bhishma who intended to marry her to his brother, King Vichitra. Her heart was given to another and she rejected the proposal. General Bhishma then released her but her lover refused, saying that she was handled by another man.

The rejected Princess then returned to Bhishma and requested marriage. She explained, "My lover rejected me, saying that you touched me while transporting me to marry your brother. Now I am without honor. It is your interference. No one will marry me after I was kidnapped by you. I am attracted to you and in consideration you should accept me."

Hearing this proposal, Bhishma blushed, but he told the Princess that marriage was out of the question since he took a vow of celibacy. To his mind, there was no possibility of taking a wife. He could not ruin his fame as an avowed celibate in a royal family.

Amba regretted this. She backed away, feeling dishonored. She went to the Himalaya Mountains to develop power to take revenge. She appealed to some senior hermits. They introduced her to a warrior-sage named Parshram. He listened to her story and decided to appeal to Bhishma, who was his former student.

When they met, Parshram asked Bhishma to take Amba because the lady had no other recourse. True to vows, Bhishma rejected the offer. Parshram, who taught Bhishma battle tactics in Bhishma's boyhood days, told his former student to prepare for a fight. He said, "Since you disregard me, since you aggravated this lady and twisted her destiny, I will punish you fittingly. Get armor. Defend yourself immediately."

The two fought but initially neither could defeat the other. In one encounter, Bhishma struck Parshram with a weapon and the teacher became unconscious. They parted, separating in peace. Parshram then explained to Amba that he could not subdue Bhishma. Hearing this, the Princess went to a more remote part of the mountains. She practiced sensual deprivation with intentions of killing Bhishma. She managed to invoke the deity Shiva. Amba asked Shiva for a male form which was capable of defeating Bhishma. The deity assured that in the next birth she would get a masculine body. By that arrangement she took birth as Princess Shikhand and then became a male warrior after her gender was exchanged for the masculinity of Stuna.

A borderline lesbian who plays the part of a male might well abandon that relationship where she has to act as if she were a male when she knows well that she is not equipped with a male body. In some cases, however, women take help from gadgets. They buy artificial organs which are strapped to their bodies. They use vibrators which are used in place of a male part.

A woman who wants to play the part of a male could well get out of a lesbian relationship and marry a man she could dominate. In that way she could behave aggressively during sexual acts, and could be domineering in domestic affairs.

The effeminate homosexual

In the case of the man who plays the part of the female to another male, he should consider that he wants a female body and that he was denied that preference by the objections of fate.

A man who plays the part of a woman must consider that what he needs is not a male partner but a woman's body. I cited the story of Princess Shikhand in which Stuna exchanged his male body for her female one. He did this by his supernatural power. Others may adjust that by transmigration adjustments.

If one is in a male body and one feels that one should be female, it is an indication that one's subtle body is female. By chance, one took a male form. Therefore one does not need a male companion for homosexuality since such a role might imperil one in the hereafter and cause one to again assume an undesirable destiny.

A man who plays the role of a woman in homosexual relationship cannot bear a child for the other partner. He should realize that the male body is frustrating. If he feels that such a frustration is an advantage, since there would be no pregnancies, he should consider that even though pregnancy is inconvenient, for reproduction it is necessary.

A person who plays the part of a female in a homosexual relationship, but who could get out of it if he chooses and who could endure a marriage relationship with a woman, should by all means abandon the same-sex situation. He should be courageous enough to consider the situation firmly and avoid risking haphazard rebirths.

Being the husband of a woman and being womanish in part, is not such a difficult situation to be in because one can be a husband and be effeminate too.

In some cases a wife takes a domineering role in decision-making and even in sexual contact. There are situations of wives who are aggressive in heterosexual relationships. They commandeer sexual acts. Therefore a man who has a tendency to be a female can find facility for that in a male-female relationship. He need not be a homosexual since a domineering woman or a sexually-aggressive female would serve his needs.

The more-emotional less-aggressive lesbian

It used to be that a woman who played the part of a female in a lesbian relationship and who made no contact with males, could not bear children, but with the advances of medical science this is no longer true. Such a woman may now enjoy the advantage of child-bearing. Doctors use artificial insemination, a technique practiced successfully on animals for many years, and now being administered upon request in women. But as Nature would have it, at the publication of this book, males who want to be females and who take hormone treatments, are still unable to carry a fetus in the body.

Lesbian women who play the part of women in the woman-to-woman relationship, can order their would-be children from a medical institution, where they are artificially inseminated with semen from a donor. Thus they become pregnant and bear children. The two women involved may register themselves as the parents of the child produced.

However, such a woman should know that what she requires is semen from the body of the woman she loves. Since that body is incapable, she has, by the grace of medical science, taken semen from a donor she may not know or love. Thus what she requires is that her womanly companion should get a male body which can manufacture sperm. She should consider this and bring to mind the prospects in future lives.

Alternately, a borderline lesbian who plays the part of a female may abandon the lesbian relationships and find or attract a man who is tender like a woman. She may find a man who is affectionate and endearing like a female.

Bisexual males

A borderline homosexual is one who might well take to a heterosexual relationship and contend with it. In other words, his capacity as a homosexual could easily be neutralized. He could be fulfilled through heterosexuality. However, such a person might need encouragement to take that step. Many homosexuals are borderline cases, persons who picked up the habit by chance in schools, gyms, boarding houses, prisons and other places, just circumstantially. One man I knew told me that while in prison he assumed homosexuality because under the circumstances, it was the only way to sexually express himself. After he was released, without regrets, he abandoned the gay lifestyle.

A man who acts out the manly role in a homosexual

relationship and who is a borderline, needs to consider that the only advantage to being in that relationship is the avoidance of the responsibility for children. Since men who play the part of women in such relationships are emotionally-inclined, just as women are, there is no advantage in the emotional sense since an effeminate man will play the womanly role and relate to his male lover as much as a woman would. The avoidance is one of responsibility for children only.

One may then analyze why one avoids that liability and of course, such an inquiry needs to be deep. In any case, to begin the consideration, one should consider that childhood life is necessary for all material bodies. Since someone must take the role of a parent, the responsibility is a necessity.

A borderline homosexual as described may be fearful of being mistreated or abused by women. That person may subconsciously carry that fear from a past life. Instead of entertaining homosexuality as an alternative, he should consider developing heterosexual relational skills.

Masturbation

Another behavior is masturbation. Regardless of whether one was introduced to this habit or whether one discovered it, one should consider its elimination. Some persons were introduced to such habits and others discovered the technique.

For instance, one's friend or sibling might introduce such a habit. I knew a young lady who came for yoga lessons. She had recently abandoned a lesbian relationship. When asked how she began such a life, she said it was introduced by her sister. Initially she was uncomfortable with it. Eventually she stopped and began to masturbate, a habit she learnt in the lesbian interchange.

A man who marries a woman who is habituated to

masturbation, may find that the woman is sexually dissatisfied if she does not masturbate during or after sexual entries or if the man does not assist by fondling her to induce climax.

For males, masturbation discharges sexual energy. In the animal world, a sexually-tensed bull may mount a male animal, or even an inanimate object, just to relieve its body of seminal pressure. Thus for males, the problem of masturbation can be solved by decreasing the body's production of semen or by decreasing the sexual stimulation that one is exposed to.

For instance, if a man sees a pornographic video, he may become sexually-excited. If he cannot have intercourse, he may be forced to masturbate. Therefore one should not view pornographic media. Another example is diet. If one eats oily foods and takes more oil into the body than necessary, the seminal vesicle may be swollen with fluids. One may have sex dreams.

Another example is that of a monk who likes to speak with women. Such a man will invariably be forced to masturbate to expel the semen that swells his seminal passages when he enjoys the face of females or hears female voices and becomes affected lustily. Since he cannot engage in intercourse, he might masturbate. The same applies to homosexual monks who get arousal from attraction to males.

Masturbation in females is more complex than masturbation in males. Female bodies are designed to create embryos from implanted semen. But the female form also has the facility to discharge fluids through clitoris and G-spot excitation. A female who is habituated to masturbation should review her past to determine how she began the practice.

Chapter 10
Comprehending Sex Desire

Honest assessment of sex desire

To integrate sex desire, one needs to analyze the following:

- *sexual impulsiveness*
- *the sweetness of indulgence*
- *the need for social approval*
- *the inability to convince a partner to look at intercourse objectively*
- *trends which dictate the continuation of intercourse in elderly years*

For males, sexual impulsiveness begins at puberty when the male body exhibits sexual tendency in the form of erection, secretion of a fluid from the prostrate gland, and the manufacture of semen in the testes. In the female form this is experienced as development of breasts, the initiation of menses, the manufacture of ova and the production of hormone secretions in the vagina.

It used to be that a human child was caught off guard by these bodily changes but nowadays children get information in schools long before these features manifest. Still, even in the modern setting, the actual experience causes astonishment. This is because the entity forgot past lives in which the same experience was derived.

Sexual impulsiveness is compulsive. It drives the gross and subtle bodies to break social taboos. In youth when puberty manifests, there is astonishment which changes into acceptance of the urge and also into a belief that the urge is insurmountable.

The first stage in comprehending sexual experience is to reduce participation. One must at least feel that there is a chance that one can contain the urge. The sweetness of indulgence is a barrier to proper evaluation. There is a relationship between the sweetness of it and our hopelessness as prisoners of intercourse. So long as we are overwhelmed by the pleasure we cannot be objective to it. The enjoyment should be assessed, broken down into parts, and then reviewed as to its real value.

In sugar there are component parts, each of which is not sweet in itself, each of which would be rejected if it were taken by itself. There is carbon, hydrogen and oxygen. None of these by itself makes for a sweet taste. In the sexual indulgence, such an analysis may reveal that the pleasure is a mixture of various forces.

There is an uneasiness one experiences if one promises to control indulgence and then finds that one must by impulse, indulge more frequently. One may vow to have intercourse once per month or even to have no intercourse at all, never ever again. One may at the time of the commitment, actually feel empowered to complete the obligation. But one might later experience a compelling need for intercourse anyway. Subsequently, one may develop guilt feelings for having broken the commitment.

Actually no one with knowledge about the compulsion of sexual nature would take such a vow. If one takes the vow and breaks it, one was ignorant of the strength of sex desire at the time of the promise.

Sex desire is so innate to a human psyche, that to take a vow to cease it, is for most people, a show of arrogance. First one must realize one's limitations. Sex desire is the most intense pleasure in the material world, undoubtedly. Nature is supportive of it. To transcend it is near impossible.

One should come to terms with the inability to convince a partner to look at intercourse objectively. Despite the pleasure, contempt or disrespect may arise from intercourse. Any time there is intercourse a certain disrespect may follow because one partner may feel that the other was beastly and indulgent. One partner may like the other for participating but at the same time there might be rejection.

Some persons get disgusted with an indulgent partner, then link with another companion and start an indulgence all over again. Thus one must be careful that one does not leave a sex-crazed lover, and then accept a new companion and repeat the history once again.

In India there is a discipline called tantra which is designed for usage by couples who desire to curb indulgence. Success on that path is uncertain. Many persons who do tantric practice do not advance but eventually become even more involved. Or they may separate from spouses and wander here and there, forming new attachments all over again.

Self-image

For monitoring sexual expression, one should have a threefold self-image consisting of:
- *what one is*
- *what one was*
- *what one might become*

What *one is* has to do with honest self-assessment of the present condition, with full understanding of faults and shortcomings. What *one was* has to do with knowing how one improved through discipline. What *one might be*, is related to one's idea of what one would be in the perfected stage. For the most part, one's view of one's potential is speculative.

Having an idea of what one should be and what one lacks, is important in sexual expression. Without self-assessment, one cannot be motivated to strive. For Instance, this writer spoke to several persons about monitoring sexual expression. Many of them simply smiled as if they were disinterested or to indicate that such an idea is for monks, nuns and elderly persons. They felt that they might try for sexual restraint after 55 or 60 years of age, not when their bodies were youthful and full of vigor. The fact is, however, that unless one strives while the body is youthful, one will make no progress later because the developed sexual interest will prevail.

Semen emittance results in drowsiness and a general lack of enthusiasm, at least until the energy is restored in the body. After semen expulsion, sleep overcomes the brain. The life force slows down thinking activity due to low power level in the spinal column. It is a tiring process to say the least but if a religious man thinks that he is above sex desire, he should question himself:

- *Who was my wife in the immediate past life?*
- *How many wives have I had in past lives?*
- *Have I, since eternity, had sexual relationships only with one female?"*

A religious woman can ask herself the converse as well, as to whether her current husband was the only husband in all past lives, in all phases of previous conscious existence.

Once one begins to understand this inconsistency due to varied, haphazard transmigrations in different bodies, different families and cultures, different places and times, one cannot help but be humbled in self-esteem.

The questions are:

- ***Even if I married this person before having intercourse, did my subtle body not experience intercourse before?***
- ***When I define a chaste body, what do I describe?***
- ***Is it a chaste physical or subtle form?***

If I control the physical body but am oblivious to the activities of the subtle form in dreams, then my behavior is contrary on the subtle level. I should be conscious on the subtle plane.

When I consider how many millions upon millions of bodies I took in complete ignorance and how many sexual contacts I had with many other bodies, I cannot afford to fake a chaste self-image. One who understands reincarnation, will not deny that the subtle body is impulsive, flirtatious and vice-prone.

In the analysis I can review myself:

- ***How many sexual organs have I used? In how many bodies?***
- ***How many sexual contacts have those bodies made?***

While transmigrating I focus on youthful bodies, to exploit sensual delights. When as juveniles we reach reproductive maturity, we go for the prize pleasure of sexual indulgence.

As babies we enjoyed milk from a mother's body, from a soft protrusion called a breast. Then we craved sweet foods. Anything sweet pleased us even if our teeth decayed and our nerves vibrated in hyperactivity. When the toddler stage passes, one rushes into the sexual stage all over again as we did in previous lives. After years of indulgence the body becomes worn and the sexual organs lose sensitivity, the man's organ being limp and the woman's stretched, shriveled and leathery. Then we regret senility. But the show is still on. As a last resort for something to cling to; we look to the mature bodies of youths and to visual and written media. We may stand as seniors taking respect, even though we are worthy of rejection and disrespect.

The design of the subtle and gross bodies, make it difficult to regulate sex. In the effort at restraint, one will invariably regress. One will fall back, indulge again, strive again and then push oneself forward again.

Even if one partner becomes detached, that person will be dragged back repeatedly. Each time one should study the situation and determine how one could effectively resist.

When one sees nudity, when one is under covers and feels the warmth of a partner's body, one cannot resist. Inevitably there is arousal and contact.

We should study the situation carefully and realize that at the time of death one departs the body and leaves the world behind. Then the search for a new gross body begins. Of course we do not remember how we left an old body, or how nature used the psyche to create the one we now possess.

First of all one has to take shelter of a sexual contact before one can get a body. First we are squirted as semen into the birth canal. Then we are housed in the uterus which is a deeper part of the mother's sexual system. Finally we are delivered from the same channel. We come out as a baby through the same place that our father's organ entered to implant us in the mother's body.

Once delivered, the mother usually keeps us on her lap and near her breasts. These areas are extensions of the sexual facility. While growing up, infants are usually drawn to their mother's laps and unconsciously become attached to the same means of sexual intercourse and birth delivery.

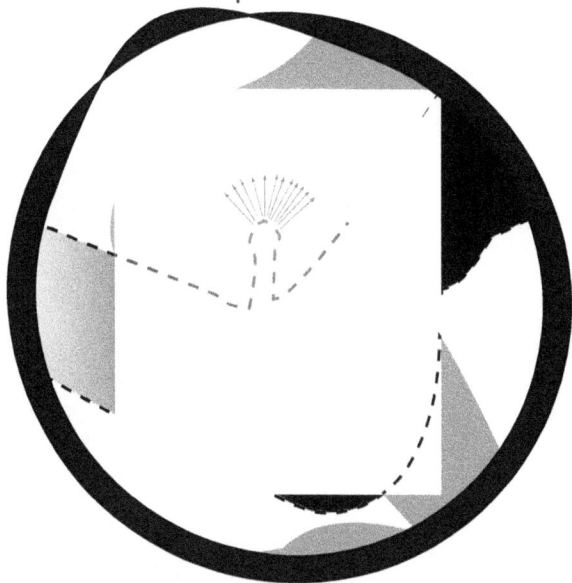

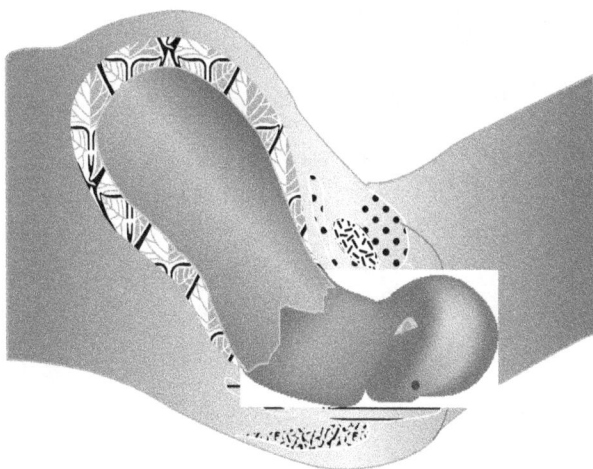

Chapter 11
Organs and Influences

The organs

Apart from the personality, the nature and the various bodies of our transmigrations, we have to deal with the sexual organs. Generally we consider what might be called the whole person, the human being, the individual, but strictly speaking, our idea of this is fallacious. What we regard as the human being is a combination of many factors. The soul, person or individual being, is part only. In the conditioned stage the soul is a small part indeed. It is not small in terms of energy provision but it is so in terms of the way it is utilized and driven by impulsions.

As one becomes increasingly enlightened, one must of necessity become increasingly perceptive. One should sort everything, understanding the various factors. One should reach a stage of knowing that the sexual organ is possessed of its own power, its own attractive force.

In the beginning of this realization one understands that the sexual organs run their own show, develop their own arousal, and move human bodies at will by urges. For instance, a man may walk down a city street without any thought of sexual indulgence. He may not be a sexually-inclined person. He may not be a masturbator. This fellow may not view sex videos, but somehow as he walks along, he may notice a sexually-appealing lady. The lady may not notice him. She may walk ahead without realizing his presence. Still, the man may feel irresistibly attracted to her torso. It is as though he was compelled to place his attention there. His eyes and head may remain focused there as if he was compelled by a force.

In that case, what attracted him? Since the lady, the soul in that body, was for the most part, unaware of the attraction, what attracted him? Was there another person in her torso? What force in her form held his attention?

The sexual part itself is possessed. When one realizes this one gives up the idea that the soul in the female body deliberately charms men. In fact, such a soul who exposes her body or wears sexually-suggestive clothing is being held captive in the castle of the body, under strict control, as a prisoner who must comply with sexual forces which inhabit the form.

In addition there is another factor in the construction and operation of a female body. By nature, sexual restraint may increase the sex drive. Indulgence increases the drive in the sense of uncontrollable craving. Restraint increases it in terms of increasing the lusty force by the increase of stored hormones.

If a woman restrains from indulgence her organ may be reinvigorated. The walls of the vagina may become refreshed, closing in tighter. Secretions in the organ may be thicker. The heat within the organ may increase. That will increase desire.

Subsequently, the pleasure will be so intense that the male will feel as if his entire gross and subtle bodies are consumed by pleasure. When the act is over, he will lay like a log, practically dead and lifeless. The female may not be satisfied. She may think,

"He has no zip. Just when I began, he ended. He climaxed too quickly. I have not enjoyed the pleasure. This man is worn out. Now I am ready, his instrument became floppy."

Let us try to understand this by contrasting the opposite situation where there is too much indulgence, as in the case of young women who have sexual intercourse practically every night. Some women have a vagina with worn-out walls because of the constant insertion of a male organ. The secretions are greatly decreased and thinned out due to over-use. As a result the vagina does not hug the male organ tightly and the intercourse is unfulfilling and sloppy. Still there is craving because that is the nature of the affair. Sex is like that—sex, sex and more sex, even though the organs have reduced fulfillment.

The predominating deity

On the psychic level the various parts of the body have predominating deities who are supernatural people who regulate the use of the organs. As soon as one increases psychic perception one may see these manipulators. For instance, there is a supernatural person who escorts and directs departed souls into would-be parent bodies. The idea is that once the ancestors gets into the body of a parent, they turn into impulses. They are experienced as urges for sexual pleasure. The would-be father's genital becomes aroused. This causes the man to visualize intercourse. Under that pressure sexual activity is initiated and the man ejaculates. The entities who are emitted without entering a fertile woman re-enter the same or some other male body to try again for a birth opportunity.

If the man becomes resistant, and if the disembodied entities find that they cannot enter his psyche because of an effective celibate approach, they will enter his wife's body and pressure him through his wife's emotions and through his familiarity with his wife's sexual parts. This involves memory of past sexual indulgence, and having to see his wife in the nude or in sexually-suggestive clothing, until at last his determination is broken and he participates in the act, thus ejaculating semen.

When entering the wife's sexual parts, the souls requiring rebirth enter the pleasure nerves in her subtle and gross bodies. These nerves encircle the sexual organ of the female.

Freedom from this possession in a female body only comes about by elimination of the lusty energy in the lower part of the body. This lusty force is experienced in the nerves of the breasts, pubic, thigh and buttocks areas.

Food and association

Partners should check to see how foods affect sex desire. If certain foods increase agitation, they should note these. If other foods increase resistance, they be aware of these. They should observe the effect of the time of eating. If by eating late at night they feel the need for more indulgence, that should be considered.

If one notices that by retaining stools, one has a tendency to think of sexual indulgence, one should consider that.

These may seem to be matters of little significance but in sexual expression even the little effects are no small concern. With sex, a small trigger, any slight urge or cause, could develop into a compulsory incidence.

A woman should observe the relationship between the need for intercourse and the menstrual cycle. A woman should know which part of the menstrual cycle is most impulsive.

The partners should observe how certain friends of the family cause an increase in the need for intercourse. The male should note how other women are attracted to him and how their association is sometimes completed by intercourse with his wife. The woman should observe how her attraction to other men requires her to have more frequent contact. Both husband and wife should observe how their minds and emotions are practically pulled out of them and into the organs during sexual indulgence, especially during orgasm. They should gage the degree of impulsion.

Once they decide to regulate indulgence by mutual observation and abstinence, they should observe how small their determination is, when compared to the lusty force. They should realize that they will be forced to break their determination periodically. Still, they should also take positive hope in the fact that the indulgences are farther and farther apart. Instead of twice per night, it may decrease to once per night, then every other night, then once per week, then bi-weekly, then monthly, then bi-monthly, then once every three months, then bi-yearly, then once per year, then gradually decreased to nil, with no regrets.

After every rainy season there will be mosquitoes. At the end of a dry spell, the weeds will sprout again. After restraining for a year, even for two years, sex desire will arise again. The partners might find they must indulge again. Still they should be observant of the forces which push them through the act. In this way by a series of abstinences, a series of indulgences, a series of restraints and a series of more indulgences, they may continue the effort, always applying restraint, never giving up even when they are forced into contact.

The partners should discuss their reunion hereafter.

- *Will they meet again?*
- *Will they meet in a higher world, or on this planet, or in a lower species of life?*

In this way they can begin thinking in the long range and perhaps realize that their relationship would improve if they ceased the sexual contacts altogether. If a couple wants to go to the higher worlds together, they must of necessity, get rid of the idea of vulgar sexual entries.

The husband and wife should decrease lusty advances as much as possible. They should not in turn feel that something is lacking. They should realize that they endeavor for a higher aim. They will become closer in the spiritual way in real terms, forsaking the gross bodily level. The material body is not the personality. It is only a channel for the energy of the personality. The affectionate embraces or sexual linkage of one human body with another is not a pure communication from soul to soul. Soul actually means the core-character in the body.

Partners who live together and want to work to increase spiritual sexual expression, need to discuss character contact as contrasted to sex organ contact. They need to realize that character contact is service-oriented while sex contact is enjoyment-oriented. Life is focused on enjoyment but if one works directly for enjoyment one gets enjoyment initially and then much responsibility, while if one focuses on service, one gets character fulfillment which is a higher form of enjoyment. Character fulfillment restores self-respect and raises the level of consideration.

One needs to discuss the increase of gray hairs, loose teeth, the loss of youthful appearance, the appealing, enjoyable but ugly-looking female part and the dangling, out-of-place, demanding male organ. One should see that the old bodies of one's parents are a sample of what one's youthful form will degrade to in a few years. One will, more than likely, have all the aches and pains that most elderly bodies endure. One should note brain dullness which comes on with old age and the loss of confidence which develops as a result of menopause and impotence.

Progressive partners should discuss that intercourse stains the mind with the memory of vulgar acts and puts the being squarely on the animal plane, thus risking a descent to lower rebirth in the next life. One needs to consider that if one passes from the body with sexual thoughts, one will carry that tendency to the next baby form and will focus on sexual contact again, thus repeating the history.

Chapter 12
Digestive System

One cannot control the stomach or intestines absolutely because these organs of the body are controlled directly by the life force and not by the soul. If one wants to control the tongue, belly and genitals to a greater degree, one has to begin with controlling the time of eating, and the items eaten. One should study physiology to understand the bodily machinery, and take steps to cooperate with it for the efficiency of digestion, excretion and sex control. In the legend of Puran, when that king was on the verge of dying, the life force became tired of protecting the body. It could no longer maintain a healthy condition. I learn from that story that the life force fights a battle for survival for the duration of the life of the body. For the most part, it fights alone. And what about Puran, the soul? What does it do? Well, it enjoys itself. It enjoys childhood, youth, sexual maturity and even seniority. It sees no necessity to assist the life force which dutifully protects the body. As a result, that energy becomes worn out and eventually the brain becomes senile when the life force can no longer energize and protect it from disease.

Since the soul is reluctant to help the life force to maintain the body and since the soul is naturally an enjoyer, it should make a deliberate effort to curb its enjoying tendency, or it will be imperiled in old age and may have unfavorable circumstances in the next body.

Diet

One should gage climatic influence. The spring and fall seasons induce lusty vibrations in mammals. The fall or autumn is the time of the cool influence. At that time a mammal's body seeks heat. This heat may be found by sexual linkage through which one senses one's bodily heat as well as the heat in the body of a mate. The life force at the base of the spine produces heat by a mixture of various types of fluids and gases. This fire at the base of the spine is called kundalini compressed force. It is felt as warmness in the belly, genital and anal areas.

During sexual intercourse, this heat increases. When the body is youthful, the heat is intense. When the body ages the heat is reduced, so much so that an old man who has intercourse with a young woman might feel that the temperature in her sexual organ practically burns his instrument. On the other hand, an elderly woman having sexual intercourse with a young man might be surprised to find out how hot his instrument is. But a youthful couple finds great pleasure in the mutual heat of the organs. In the case of the female, the heat is recessed in the entry and in the case of the male, the heat is first felt by the flush of blood which inflates the instrument to erection. It

is felt again as the rush of seminal energy which is
expelled from the body.

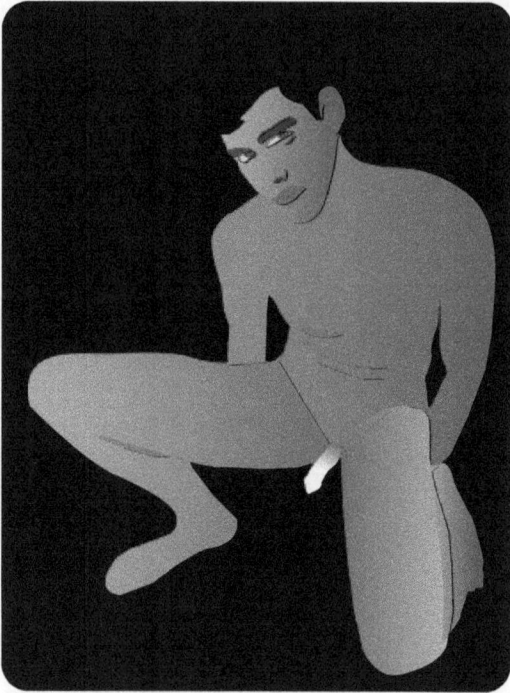

In the fall season when the weather cools, human beings, deer, dogs and other creatures may seek out each other to share body heat. This promotes intercourse.

Another important aspect of the seasonal changes is the influence of the weather on the excretory functions of the body. When the weather cools down, the digestive and excretory functions operate slower. When this occurs, sex desire automatically increases. Any time the mind lodges an interest in the stomach and intestines there is a risk for increased sexual interest. Some couples meet at a restaurant, eat and drink and then go off to have sex or go off thinking of it.

sex you!

The mind must be deliberately kept away from the belly and lower intestines. This implies reduction in eating, which results in reduction of bodily waste, resulting in reduction of the mind's preoccupation in the lower trunk of the body.

In a cold climate when the food enters the lower intestines, it takes longer to pass through that area. This sluggishness results in increased mental interest in the belly which draws the mind and life force to the sex organs, causing an increased interest in sexual expression.

For people who live near the equator, the changes in weather are not so extreme, but even these people have to deal with the cooling factor during the rainy season and when the earth tilts on the vernal and autumnal equinoxes. In coastline areas, the cooling ocean breezes that come inland as well as moist, cooling breezes during the rainy season, cause an overall increase in sexual attraction and indulgence. One should observe such influence.

There is a connection between the anus and the genitals, between passing waste and discharging sexual secretions. This should be considered in trying to understand sexual expression. It requires observation of the body and its impulsions.

The connection between sexual indulgence and passing waste from the body can be observed easily, when one notices that after sexual intercourse, stools pass easier. For instance, if a man passes stools, let us say for example, at 6:00 a.m. usually, he may pass that stool earlier the previous night if he has intercourse. In other words sexual intercourse causes increased circulation and increased muscular activity in the large colon and rectum. In fact, in the developed countries, some doctors question constipated patients about sexual activity. If a patient has infrequent intercourse, a doctor may tactfully suggest that the rate of contact be increased. This verifies a relationship between vigorous sexual activity and evacuation. It is not unusual to find that a woman or man has to interrupt sexual contact to pass urine or stool. The emotional force activates the waste functions when sexual contact is made.

The energy which stimulates the sex area is assisted by carbon dioxide, liquor, marijuana, oily foods, flesh foods, peppers and other types of foods. One should realize this. One should avoid peppery foods. Pepper in the mouth means pepper in the sexual organ which may cause increased sexual activity.

Liquor may promote sexual activity. Carbon dioxide is always being produced by cellular activity. Therefore the digestive, sexual and excretory functions of the body which in part use this energy, will go on. It cannot be stopped but improved circulation greatly decreases it. Through improved circulation the worn-out blood cells return to the heart to be brought to the lungs where the

sex you!

carbon dioxide is expelled, being exchanged for fresh air.

When there is foreplay in sex, sweet romantic dealings, the waste gases in the blood stream react in the lower portion of the body. The woman's organ becomes slimy and warm, the man's becomes firm and is poised for insertion. His seminal tubes are laden with slimy secretions. This is conducted by the lust hormones in the body.

Chapter 13
Breaking the Habit

Non-hypocritical sexual restraint greatly enhances one's evolutionary status in terms of the cultivation of higher habits which lead to the higher worlds, whereas a lack of it is conducive to reincarnation in the lower worlds.

In the male body a lack of continence draws the life force into the genitals which act as a funnel to channel sexual energy out of the body.

In the female form, the sexual opening acts with suction force to draw seminal energy out of the male form into the female body, but the female system also has an outward expression which can be triggered.

sex you!

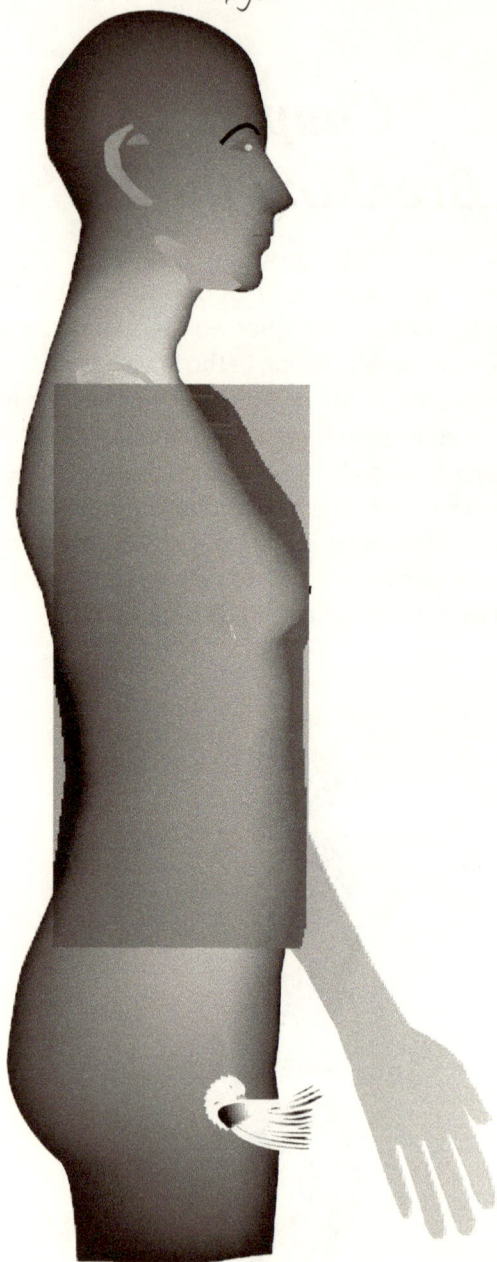

As the seminal fluids are drawn up psychically into the female form, female sexual hormones travel to the womb to meet with the incoming semen. The result for a potent man and fertile woman, is the production of an embryo. This translates into responsibility.

One should realize that sexual pleasure is not a fair reward for the time it takes to raise progeny. Though a necessity, the pleasure of one sexual act is not ample reward for a resultant pregnancy. For those who are not satisfied with the one act and who continue having intercourse during the pregnancy and during the lactation period when the child is breast-fed, there is necessity to realize that the additional pleasure derived is not worth it because such indulgence is an exploitive activity that may bear undesirable consequences in the form of hardships imposed by destiny in this or future lives. Ideally, the act of producing progeny should commence and be terminated with one sexual intercourse. The satisfaction of that intercourse should be seen as a token encouragement for the greater task ahead which is the responsibility for the upbringing of the child produced.

For those who want no child but who want the sexual pleasure or who may not want the pleasure but who must have it anyway because they simply cannot help but indulge, they should regard the indulgence as an impulsion.

A good birth in the next life would come if one attempts sexual restraint and tries one's best to curtail gross and subtle indulgence, living without vulgarity. In the beginning this may seem to be an impossible task but step by step, one can curb the psyche.

One must make an endeavor to cause the life force to energize the brain. This is done by freeing oneself from so much involvement in the lower trunk of the body. One should free the life force from having to work overtime in the digestive track by regulating the quantity, time and frequency of meals. One must free the life force from having to maintain passionate energy in the thighs, buttocks, pubic area and breasts by uprooting mental interest in these sectors and by doing anything possible to improve the blood circulation, causing the exhausted blood in the veins to move quickly to the heart and lungs where the carbon dioxide is expelled in respiration.

For all that it is, sexual intercourse is a form of feeding, a form of eating, where the male organ tastes and eats the female one and where the female apparatus (or anus) does the same in relation to the male structure. In other words, the highly sensitive feeling cells in the organs act like tasting instruments just as specialized cells in the tongue function as taste sensors. In the genitals, however, the taste is that of pleasure energy in flesh. Through the sexual opening, the woman perceives the taste of the man's organ and the man experiences the same in reverse.

The subtle energies involved on the psychic side of intercourse, are so intense that the parties involved in an intercourse must of necessity, retract optic energy and concentrate fully on the sensations, regardless of whether it is desired or not. It draws one's attention completely away from any other objective. No other focus in the material world is so intense and demanding as sexual expression.

During intercourse, the average human being, even the religious type, may surrender fully to the sexual experience. When the rush of pleasure comes, the soul may be compelled to give itself fully to the experience. In the intensity, practically all the cells of the body participate and every section of the mind and feelings become involved. In that way the collective cell consciousness contributes to the experience.

Nature organized the sexual act for the manufacture of baby forms, using the parental forms as the prototype from which the infant body would be copied. In a sexual act where there is no progeny, nature's main feature, reproduction, is frustrated.

Blood plasma is manufactured in the bones. It is based on bone marrow. The longest bone in the body is the thigh bone, and there is a bone grid in the body in the form of the rib cage which protects vital organs. Much blood is manufactured by the thigh bone, and also by the rib cage but if this energy is used for sexual indulgence, it means that the thighs serve the sexual organs. The rib cage would be there only to provide enriched plasma, not to the vital organs which it encloses, but to our sentiments for sexual love.

Intercourse which does not produce a child is excessive. Furthermore, intercourse which produces children but also causes further intercourse while the child is in the womb of the mother and which causes more intercourse while the child is taking milk from the mother's breast, and which causes further intercourse again after the child is no longer an infant, is impulsive.

Sexual intercourse is undoubtedly the most stubborn, most persistent vice. These bodies are born from sex, live through it, and may focus on it till death. Sexual indulgence is so powerful of an urge, that as soon as one makes progress in curbing it, as soon as one develops the idea, "I am progressing, I am no longer attracted. I transcended the need," just as one experiences this confidence, one is compelled to indulge again.

Sex in higher dimensions

While compiling notes for this book and making observations for the conclusions shared, I had some experience in a divine world where sexual companionship is enjoyed only through the eyes and presence and not through sexual organs. In those places the idea of organ penetration does not even arise in anyone's mind. The satisfaction of gender difference between male and female is lived out visually, through the face of the body.

Chapter 14
Sexual Anatomy

Sexual desire and stool retention

The connection with stools and sex desire is relevant. The lowest chakra, the base one, at the end of the spinal column, is concerned with motion, excretion and generation of heat. Traditionally this chakra is noted for its excreting function. The next chakra regulates the sexual function. It is situated so close to the base chakra that if stool is retained, much of the life force energy diffuses automatically into the sexual areas. This causes an increase in sex desire. If, as soon as the energy leaves the base, it is all but used up to process excessive food intake and to maintain solid waste, then some of the energy will not reach the brain. Much of it will be used for evacuation, sexual interest and digestion. Much of it will drift into the sexual area and promote lusty interests. This contributes to a lower energization of the brain, which is realized as drowsiness or as an impulse to tire quickly and sleep longer.

Excessive sexual desire means that the life force sends more energy to the sexual area than is required. As a result the brain will be starved of its required supply of power. This will also cause laziness, drowsiness and sleep. Apart from emitting semen from the male body and sexual secretions and menses in the vaginal passage of the female one, we have to deal with various forms of sexual excitation such as enjoying the sexual forms of others or seeing others in sexually-revealing clothing. In addition we have to deal with flirtations and romantic pulses. This causes drainage of life force energy which indirectly means that there will be less energy going to the brain.

Any part of the body which uses more energy than necessary will contribute to the drowsiness and excessive sleep which is brought on by lack of energy reaching the brain. The sexual and the excretory regions are connected. It is hard to distinguish one from the other. In fact in homosexuality, the intimacy between the sexual and the anal parts of the body are realized. Homosexuals and some females use the anus as a vagina. In fact, to some human beings, these organs are interchangeable. A homosexual commits the anus to vagina service.

Drowsiness can be reduced by ceasing sexual indulgence, carrying out prompt evacuations and increasing oxygen intake. One should make the most efficient use of the material body by maintaining it properly, allotting it the proper rest at the proper time, and by eating the proper diet.

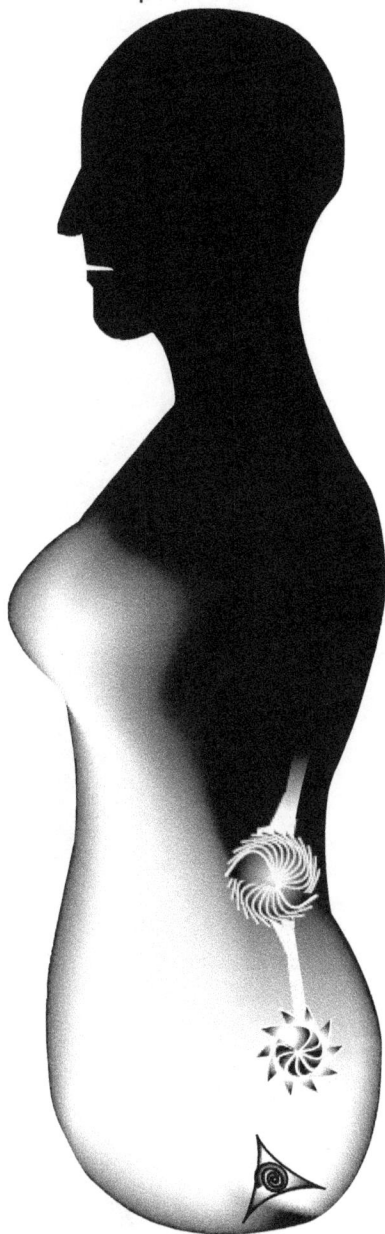

Stool retention

Deliberate or non-deliberate retention of stools, promotes dull consciousness. It makes the brain drowsy, and causes stupor and confusion of mind. This also affects the subtle body. The brain of the subtle body is experienced as the mind of the physical body.

If stool is retained, the energy reaching the brain is reduced. But the brain is also affected in another way. Its chemistry is affected by the pollutants which are ingested from stale stools which linger in the colon. These stale stools are squeezed by the colon. It extracts nutrients from the stools. These nutrients, however, are pollutants. This means that when stool is retained the brain is starved of energy and is polluted chemically by having to use polluted blood which is created by the stool-sucking action of the colon.

Sexual indulgence

The expulsion of semen is an energy loss. It causes fatigue and drowsiness. Semen and ova are important secretions. These are created in the testes and ovaries respectively. In the testes a cloudy or clear liquid is created from blood. In the ovaries a reddish liquid is produced. Both of these are pretty much the same, except that semen is more concentrated than ova. In any case, the life force expends energy in the routine manufacture of sexual secretions. After manufacture, the liquids are stored in the testes and its related tubing and in the ovaries and its related apparatus. These secretions are used in one of three ways, namely:

- *the manufacture of babies*
- *the enrichment of the blood*
- *the enhancement of romantic feelings and sexual pleasure*

In terms of fluids for the manufacture of infant forms, only one sperm is required from a man's semen and only one ovum is necessary and still the human body produces millions of sperms in the lifetime of a man and at least one mature ovum or egg per month for the fertile non-pregnant years of a female body.

For reproduction, one sperm is required and since only one sexual entry is required to produce a baby form, there is really no compelling necessity for repeated intercourse between the male and female bodies.

In direct opposition to blood enrichment by sexual restraint is sexual indulgence which discharges the refined liquids. To offer some blood in the form of semen and ova to an ancestor, for the manufacture of a body is reasonable. A new human body is worth it. To enjoy sexual indulgence and not to beget an infant form is inefficient. When the sexual energy is used for enjoying through sexual contact or through self-stimulation of the sexual organs, the bloodstream is starved of vital blood concentrate. If one indulges in ongoing, nightly, or even weekly intercourse, one robs the blood of vitality. The brain has filtering layers through which essential chemicals pass from the bloodstream. If these chemicals are used up in pleasure-yielding intercourse, one deprives the brain of energy.

One should decide either to enrich brain power through abstinence or exhaust the enjoying powers through indulgence. If one decides to enjoy through the genitals, one will have less psychic perception. If one decides in the direction of psychic development, one should reduce genital engagement.

Apart from manufacture of baby forms and enrichment of blood, sexual secretions are used for sheer pleasure. The sexual organs have straining filters that extract particular concentrates from the bloodstream. Even though some of these fluids are clear, whitish, yellowish or pinkish or bloody, still these are concentrated blood essentially. These fluids are manufactured from blood, which is manufactured in the bones of the body from bone marrow. With this in mind, we can constantly remind ourselves that when indulging, we are actually bleeding. Even though the fluids may not be red, still we are bleeding.

When a woman falls in love with a man or if she is sexually agitated at a certain time of the month, and when as a result, her vagina secretes hormones, she is bleeding. A wet dream for a man means that he has bled off highly refined blood during sleep.

Chapter 15
Life Force Operations

The rest cycle

We can understand the life force and its operation from a study of the rest cycle of the body. Let us examine what happens when the body rests. First of all, we may have dreams. Actually we always have dreams during rest but we remember only a few of them. This remembrance is related to energy efficiency. The more efficient the use of energy, the more memory a person would have of dreams.

Dreams signify our ability to function in the subtle world and in the mindscape of imagination. Both worlds, that of the subtle and that of imagination, are real to a degree, but the imagination is based on the mind's creative power, while the subtle worlds are factual dimensions. Since we can function in dreams while the body rests and then get up in the body and operate it, the implication is that our souls, our life force, and our bodies, are all different realities. If there were no life force running the maintenance of the body, it would not heal nor stay alive unless we were attentive to it.

While we dream either in the subtle world or in imagination, the life force repairs worn-out cells, rejuvenates blood, takes oxygen for itself from the lung operations, and sets the organs in order within the body. When it is finished, we find ourselves back in the body with gross perception. As a user of the body, the soul is displaced from it to allow the life force, to do its maintaining chores.

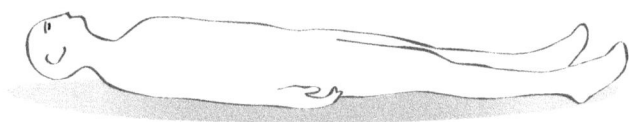

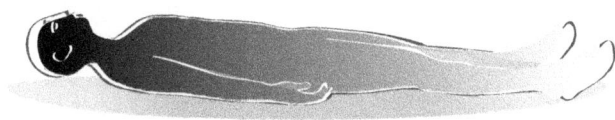

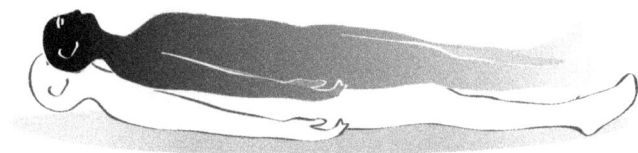

sex you!

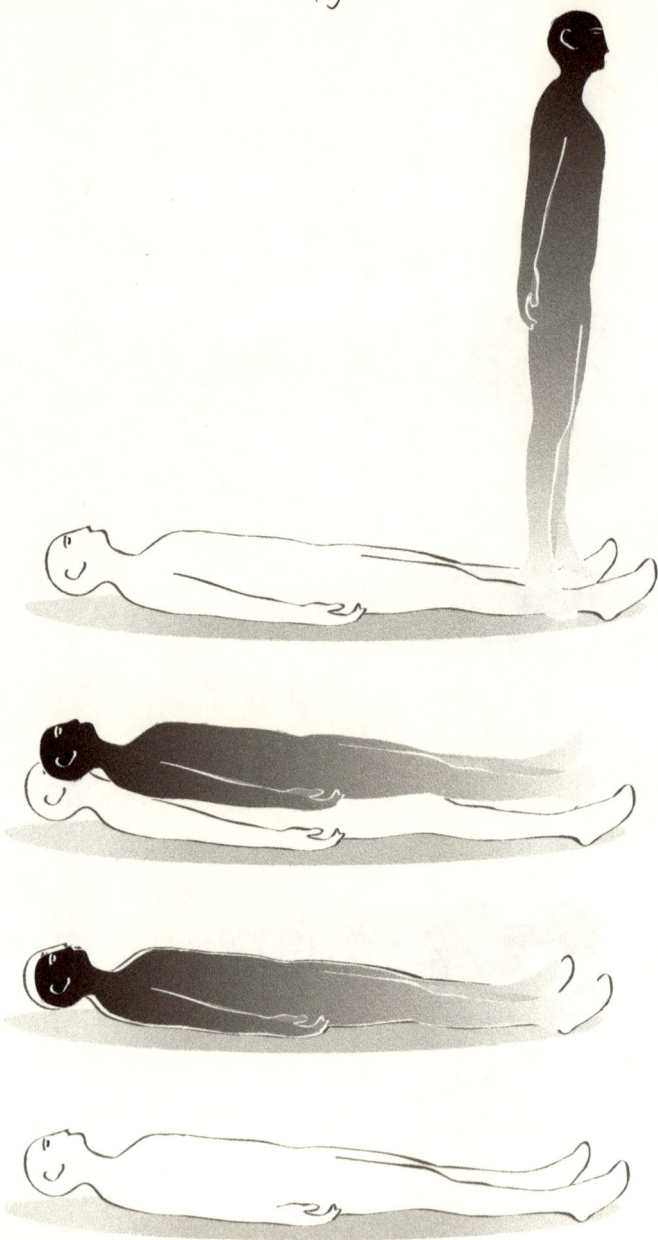

Mental energy is used by the intelligence, which monitors the five senses. Under the senses, innumerable desires are fulfilled. These psycho-physical systems depend on the life-force. As long as the life-force is there, the mind works, and under the mind, the senses operate.

The life force remains active in the body at all times. It protects the body during sleep, heals it and refreshes it by taking energy from food and breath. It distributes this breath energy to various parts of the body. We, the selves, as users and enjoyers, are hardly concerned with the body's maintenance. The life force puts us out of commission by shutting down cognitive functions in the brain. Then it goes to work on routine maintenance.

Even though we consider the body as a tool for sense fulfillment, it could not function in good health if it was not maintained by the life force. When the body becomes terminally ill, the life force senses that it can no longer operate the form. It seeks an escape, just as a serpent in the cavity of a burning tree tries to get out before it is too late.

It so happens that usually the life force becomes fatigued and panicky just before death of the body. When at last it endeavors to leave the dying body, it may be restricted. But eventually it breaks free and enters the astral world full time.

In the rest cycle, the life force reduces energy supply to the brain by decreasing the amount of electric power which goes up the spine. When the life force shuts off most of the power to the brain, the soul feels drowsy. Falling asleep only means that the means of perception to this gross world is suspended for the time being. Once this perception is lost, the life force transfers the electric power used in the brain to other parts of the body, particularly to the heart and lungs. The main interest of the life force is the lung because the lung takes in the air which surcharges blood. The heart then distributes the charged blood through the system of arteries. The main business of the heart is to pump rejected blood to the lungs and to take surcharged blood from the lungs to the other parts of the body.

The more a human being lives recklessly, the more the life force induces drowsiness and sleep, so that it can maintain the body. Without the brain a living entity cannot exploit the sensual pleasures of the body. But if the entity over-uses the brain, the system collapses and during sleep or coma, the life force attempts to refurbish the body. The body is manufactured in such a way as to limit the amount of enjoyment derived from it. Nature gave a certain authority to the life force to check us by drowsiness and sleep. This dullness of brain regulates our exploitive capacity.

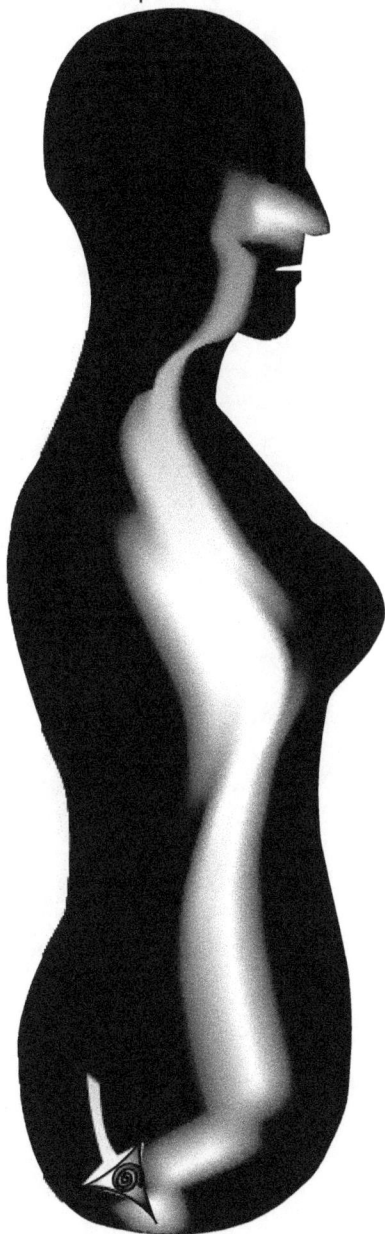

sex you!

Chapter 16
Subtle Body

Sexual expression of the subtle body

Even if one cannot perceive the subtle form, one can know it as the mind, emotions and random psychic energy. The mind is sensed by the thinking and visualization functions in the head. The emotions flow mostly through the head, chest and genital areas. Besides these, there is the life force which radiates from the sacral bone. A portion of yoga concerns itself with energization of the life force. When this energy is surcharged, one becomes capable of accurate psychic perception.

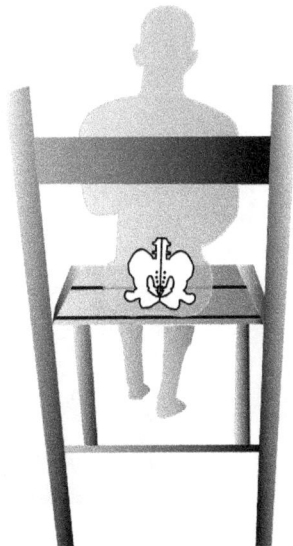

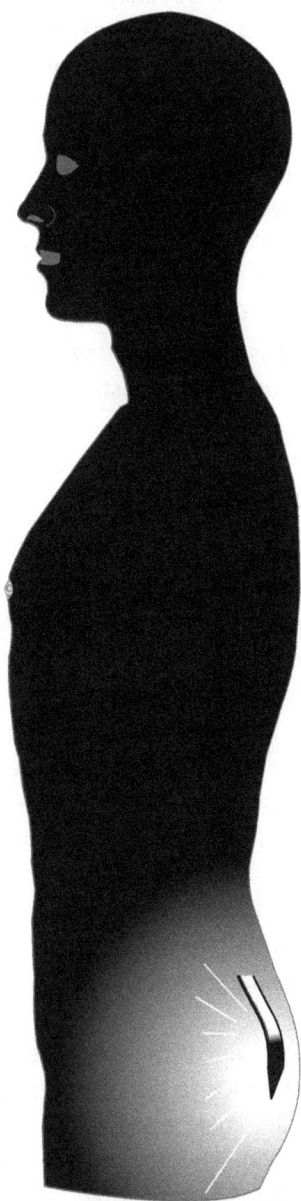

The first part of sexual abstinence concerns the physical form. So long as there is a physical body, the subtle form is, to a degree, conditioned and motivated by physical conditions. The converse is also true whereby the subtle form motivates and conditions the physical one. The energies and influences of these bodies are interchanged. Sexual restraint begins on the physical level because this is the easiest one to control. If one cannot regulate the sexuality of a gross body, one will not be able to abstain in the subtle one. The subtle one is harder to control, more impulsive, and less discriminating. If we attain gross control, we can use that resistance to monitor subtle sexual activities.

Full sexual expression

Some objective analysis is required. This is developed through detachment. With detachment one may hesitate when given opportunities for sexual indulgence. One may resist sexual proposition.

Full sexual freedom means release from the bondage of sexual attraction in the material world. In the spiritual world, there is sexuality, but it is gender based not sex organ based. Actual sexual restraint means release from mundane sexuality. It does not include release from spiritual sexuality. Spiritual sexuality does not bind anyone. It does not express itself irresponsibly. Thus there is no need for restraint in the spiritual world. But in the material world, sexual expressiveness easily turns into a liability.

Conquering the province of sexual expression means understanding the opposite sex completely. For women, it means understanding male psychology.

We acquire and relinquish many material bodies. We have intertwining relationships during many lives. It is imperative that we understand these actions. We switch partners continually in various lives.

The motive

An important part of responsible sexual expression is motive. We should gradually purify ourselves of counter-productive motives. Someone may regulate sexual expression to develop a resistance to sexual temptations. This is not a bad motive for a beginner but ultimately it is detrimental to genuine restraint.

Perfect sexual expression is attained only after we take up the practice for the sake of morality on the basis of acceptance of responsibility for progeny. Actually, the good benefits attained through responsible sexual expression are a distraction from the real reason for doing it, which is to become spiritually elevated. The modesty, the conservation of energy, the resulting steadiness of mind, all make us fit as elevated spiritual beings. That is the real foundation for restraint.

When I began abstinence, I was running away from many of the bad effects of the sexual vice. I wanted to escape from exhaustion. I tried to refurbish a run-down mental and emotional constitution. I tried to figure why orthodox methods of salvation do nothing to shake the tendency for irresponsible sexual indulgence nor strengthen against the temptations of sex attraction. Most of all I tried to restore my sense of integrity which dictated from within that I should act in a way that was honorable to my ideals. Gradually, one by one, these motives disappeared. I continued the practice for the sake of being compatible to divine beings.

It is the subtle body that we enjoy while indulging. We use the gross body for it, but it is the subtle body that provides the captivating sexual pleasure. The inclination of the subtle body which exposes us to sexual pleasure, needs to be realized.

sex you!

Even if the gross body is curbed from sexual desires, still the need for sex may remain. It will definitely be there if the subtle form is not curbed. Even if we were to remove the genitals from the gross body or if we were to do something to remove the gross sexual urge, still the subtle body will retain the desire. In practice, after one reforms the gross body one is still faced with the desires that remain in the subtle form. If the gross body is curbed, the subtle form will fulfill itself in the subtle world in dreams and visions. Once the gross body is curbed we should intensify the effort to purify the subtle form.

As long as we continue seeing others as sexual facilities, we will not be able to curb the visionary impulses of the subtle body. We have to change the assessment of sex attraction on this physical plane. As we develop and improve, we may move to higher levels and deal with the challenges that arise at each stage.

On the physical level, a male body considers a female one as a facility for deposit of sexual fluids. The female body sees the male one as an insertion pleasure tool for deposit of fluids. From either position one has to take the self away from these views and simply reduce the outlook to nature's reproductive necessity. One may become reoriented to viewing the sexual organs as utilities for dispelling urine and delivering progeny.

A boy or girl begins this life as a helpless infant, not being able to feed its body. To the infant a woman's body is a combination of a milk factory, a nanny and a source of affectionate energy. In this threatening and harsh world, the infant appreciates the mother's affection which cushions uncertainties and fears. But when the infant body reaches maturity, it begins to see the adult forms differently as the sexual drive is developed in its body. Somehow, one has to adopt that infant innocence and abandon memories of sexual activity.

For advancement of psychic sexual restraint one should disassociate from those who are habituated to the vulgar sexual behavior, as well as those who are expert at avoiding the vulgar methods but who are well-adapted to subtle flirtation. It is easy to give up the association of those who are vulgar but it is difficult to give up the company of those who control their physical sexuality but are active sexually on the psychic plane.

Chapter 17
Hellish World

I had some experiences in the astral world of a hell place, which was for sex offenders. One may reach such a hell in a moment but one crosses a great dimensional distance to get there. The subtle body is very light and flimsy. It can travel as fast as the speed of light. According to modern calculations, light crosses a distance of about 190,000 miles in one second. When the subtle body is energized like a light ray, it can transit instantly.

I went to one hellish location where there were many men and women, all using subtle bodies. We walked on a road barefooted. It was very uncomfortable. There was no way to turn around and no way out. There was a deep swamp on either side of the road. There were guards with whips all along. Everyone was compelled to move on. Some of us could hardly find our way due to diseases in our subtle bodies. Some were blind but they moved under threat of guards. Others hobbled along because their feet were diseased with sores.

At a certain point along the way, we entered a building. We began to go down and down on a staircase into a vast subterrranean cave in the planet. On either side of the staircase we saw women and men indulging in intercourse but we could not leave the stairway or stop moving to relate to them. There was a high wall. Even though we could see the indulgers we could not go over. Most of these persons were intoxicated by a drug. We kept moving. After some time the stairs began to rise and we were again on an open road surrounded by a swamp. There were men up ahead carrying huge boulders. They strained to lift these. Even though the men were some 100 feet ahead of us, we never could reach them. It seemed that as we got closer, the distance remained the same.

After this my subtle body was released and I returned to this earthly place.

Chapter 18
Progeny Management

The progeny factor has importance but only in terms of physical sexual expression. On the subtle level, progeny is not produced by sexual intercourse. And thus subtle sexual contact is not accompanied by pregnancies. In that sense, gross sexual contact is more restrictive than the subtle sexual linkage of bodies.

The desire for progeny, however, exists in the lower subtle dimensions, just as it does in this gross existence. This is one reason why we desire physical bodies even though the physical form is limiting and restrictive. In the preliminary stages of physical sexual restraint, one should bring oneself to the level of not having intercourse unless one desires progeny. Ideally, this means that every sexual act should result in pregnancy. Otherwise one should not indulge. This is a difficult concept. It is one thing to take a vow to have sexual contact only to produce children. It is an entirely different matter to manage that commitment.

Unless one comes from a family tradition in which the elders had themselves attained a high degree of physical and subtle sexual de-expression, one cannot live up to such a vow. It is imaginary for those from other traditions.

Wonderful indeed is that couple who without stress, would have sexual intercourse only when producing children, and who would only have one intercourse per child.

The sexual energies of a woman's body are also invested for nourishment. We see this in an infant's view of its mother's body. The child considers the mother's form as an affection-yielding, milk-producing personality.

Sexual contact should be a *no no*, something that we do not indulge in unless we plan to beget infants, raise them, train them until they reach maturity. If we do not want the responsibility, we should shift our minds away from contact.

A son or daughter

With the consideration of having intercourse only for the production of progeny, a question arises as to what sex the infant would be. Many ancient kings were perplexed by this and sought techniques to guarantee that their semen would produce male bodies. There is a case of King Manu, whose wife Shraddha influenced a priest to chant sounds which would produce a female baby. The priest was successful and the King was disappointed.

I feel that the sex of the infant is fated. One desires a particular sex of progeny because of crazy desires and because of wanting to control providence. It is best to allow providence to manifest itself and then strive to do one's best to raise the child produced. There is no use in a father becoming annoyed merely because his wife's body produced an infant of undesirable gender. Ancient warrior kings, however, had reason to lament about girl children. Rules of succession did not permit a princess to take ruling power. It was not practical for women to function as warriors. By those rules only a prince could assume kingly authority. Thus kings who wanted a successor were in anxiety for male heirs.

Begetting has to do with pleasing ancestors who require bodies. There is a limit to how much one can satisfy the departed elders. One requires mystic insight to see the departed souls and to know their requirements for embryos. Some of them will wait years to get a human form. When we depart from these forms, we may be in the same situation.

Once a child's body is produced, the parent requires mystic insight for directing the infant in a spiritually-beneficial way. This is why in ancient India, as a matter of tradition, parents frequently took their children to a ritual priest. They believed that an astrologer could perceive the entity's past life and give appropriate advice on methods of child care. Unless the parents get perfect advice or can see past lives directly, they cannot resolve the infant's perplexities. Unless one has mystic insight or consults with a reliable mystic, one will invariably fail at parenting. No mystically-blind parent can see how to raise a child properly and more than likely that parent will relate to the child as if he or she is its new body.

Traditionally, religious parents proudly find a priest to perform the various ritualistic ceremonies for the welfare of a child, but they are not as eager about training the infant's mind and molding the infant's behavior. The ceremonies are performed. The parents feel satisfied. Their efforts with the child end there.

Would-be children who enter the body of a celibate

Abstinence by its very nature, is a system of cheating ancestors who require bodies. We need not deny this. Those who practice partial restraint cheat as well. After all, the ancestors who are disembodied and who must take rebirth in this earthly situation, are dependent on sexually-mature relatives to beget infant forms. This means that anyone who plans to restrain, automatically plans to deprive the ancestors.

Let us say, for example, that in his lifetime a man could, if he made sexual contact within a marriage, beget at least twelve children. Then we can understand that if he is celibate, he effectively deprived twelve departed souls from getting infant forms. This is something to admit.

Needy ancestors might break the resolution of a restrained man. I used to have a problem with ancestors who entered my body hoping to get embryos. I tried many methods to exorcise them. Some worked. Some failed. After trying and trying I approached a Krishna deity. The deity said, "Transfer the entities who enter the semen. Relocate them to the subtle plane."

After getting this advice I was happy and successfully exorcized them. However, after sometime, some of the entities returned. I again went to the deity. He explained, "Only some returned. Only those whose piety is connected to your sexually-active female friends returned. If you can recognize an ancestor, transfer the person into the particular female to whom it is linked. If you do not recognize one initially, observe his or her path on a re-entry, then transfer the person to the source person's psyche."

This instruction of the deity was the complete advice. This worked fully. Later on, I developed a particular sexual control technique known as vajroli. Once I mastered this vajroli procedure, the entities no longer entered. But it took some time to develop this vajroli action. I developed a method of vajroli that was shown to me by Yogi Satyananda. He showed me this in the astral world.

However, this is only part of the solution. Both partners have to deal with outside sexual flirtations and outside subtle sexual contacts. This happens when the male sees another woman and feels a compulsion to have intercourse; or when the female sees another man and gets an inclination for contact.

Since these outside relationships are not curbed by physical restraint, one has to make the psyche immune to them by a mystic method of transferring any entities who pass through the emotions into one's body. An extra-marital flirtation means that a departed entity influences one to have an illicit intercourse. Sometimes a person leaves a legally-married spouse and accepts a new partner. Unless they use a contraceptive method or unless either of their bodies is incapable of producing children, the result is a child. This means that the partners were influenced by that child while the child was in a departed state as a spirit requiring a body.

Vajroli has two traditional methods; one is sahajoli where the urethral muscles are drawn in to stop semen discharge; the other is amaroli, where the same muscle is drawn in to retract sexual fluids.

The Krishna deity advised that if any entities entered my body from incidental or deliberate outside relationships, I should return the entities to the person from whose body that entity originated. The entity passed through the affectionate exchange between myself and the other person. This energy is usually identified as romance, love, or irresistible sexual attraction.

Chapter 19
Organ Details

There are two parts to the sexual apparatus. One is the semen or ova producing part. The other is the instrument which emits the semen or discharges unused ova. The semen-producing part is the testes. It consists of two glands which refine and filter blood. This may be easily curbed by postures and by special breath infusion practices. The ova-producing part is the ovary. This is within the female body. It refines and filters blood. This part may also be curbed by postures and breathing techniques.

Besides these glands we have to deal with the penis, the organ which becomes erect and the vagina, the passage to the uterus which is designed to temporarily house the penis and to function as a birth canal. Both of these parts operate compulsive urges. Initially one must tolerate their agitation and gradually, as one attains a degree of restraint and a confidence that the practice is effective, one can get a method for curbing the sexual appetite of the organs. They are curbed by an infusion of fresh psychic energy. They are agitated through the build-up of the lusty force which we experience as love emotions. If that energy is flushed out by psychic charges, the organs give little or no trouble.

In the male body, the glands which produce the sexual fluids for generation of baby forms are different from the part which emits the fluids. Correspondingly, in a woman's body, the ovaries are different from the vaginal passage.

An understanding of male and female anatomy helps to clarify this.

sex you!

Female Reproductive Organs

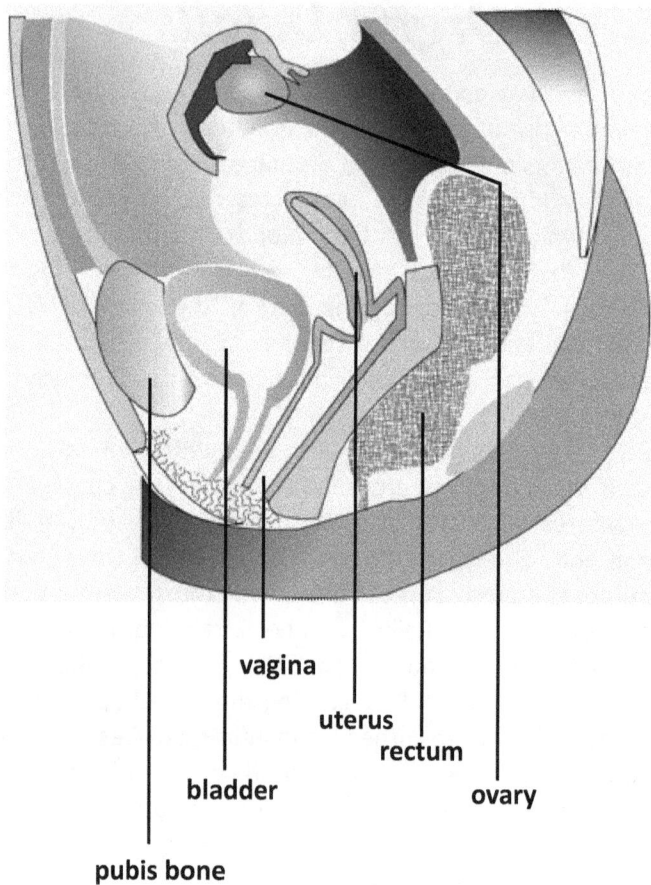

vagina

uterus

rectum

bladder

ovary

pubis bone

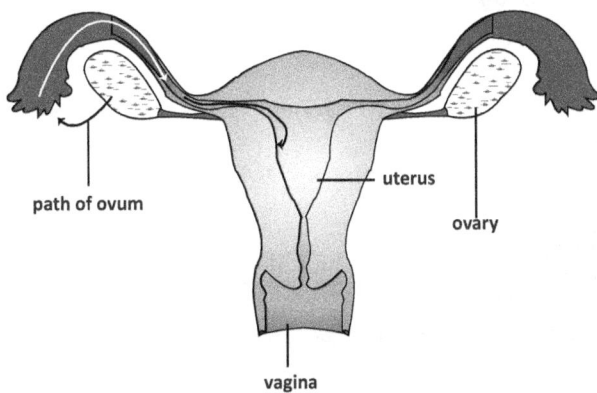

path of ovum

uterus

ovary

vagina

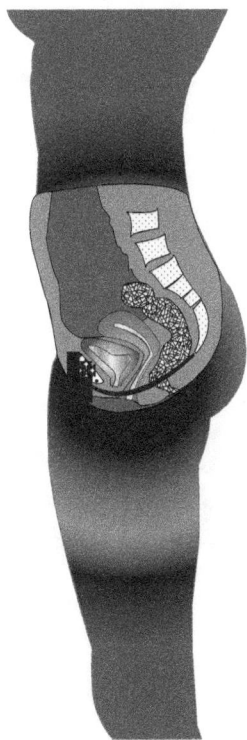

Male Reproductive Organs

bladder

passage of semen

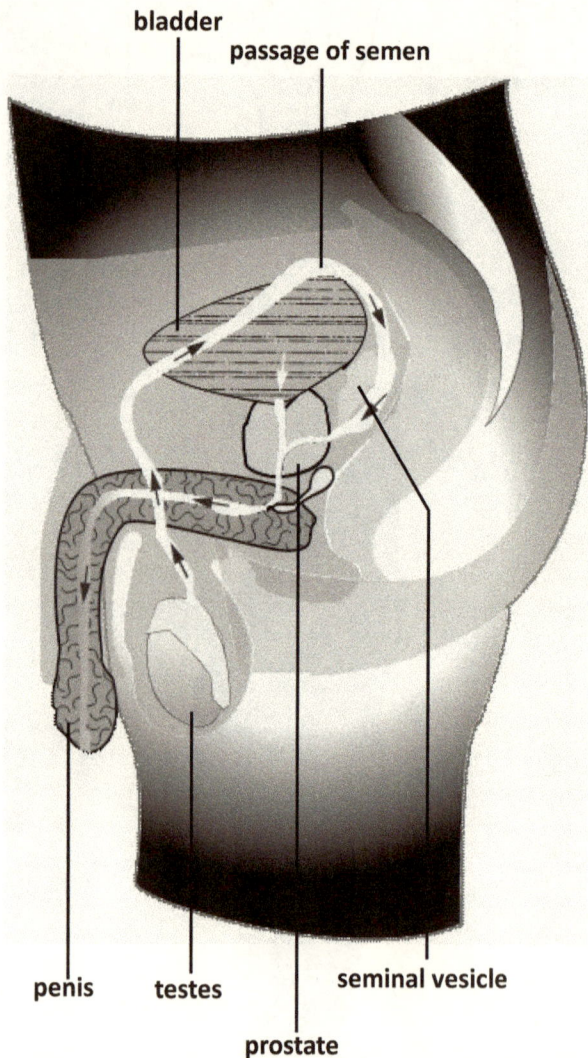

penis   testes

prostate

seminal vesicle

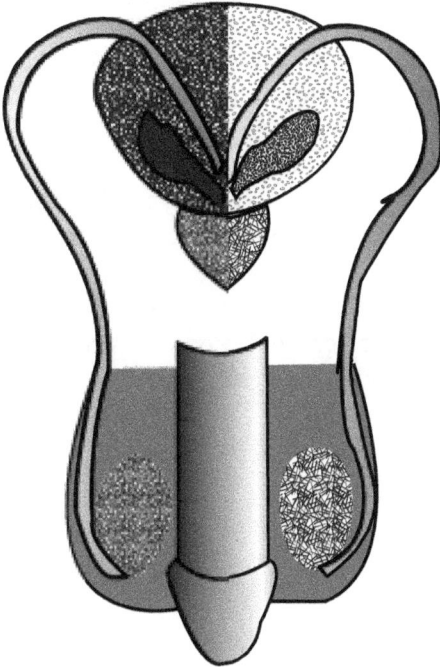

Menstruation

One should realize that the objective in sexual expression
is to get more refined semen or ova to re-enter the
bloodstream to enrich it, rather than be used in sexual
indulgences which do not produce progeny.

Many of us do not produce children but still we have
sexual intercourse rarely or frequently. Secondly, some of
us have casual intercourse without commitment to the
partner involved. If perchance children come, we neglect
them. Some others are not having intercourse due to the
status as monks or nuns. But some clergy-folk masturbate
to throw off unabsorbed fluids and secretions which build
up in the organs. Some others simply allow the secretions
to remain in the tubes and to leak from the penis or
vagina in wet dreams.

sex you!

In the case of women, they have to deal with the monthly menstrual cycle, which is the body's effort to develop and either utilize or expel egg cells. When there is a pregnancy, this cycle of expulsion of blood, sexual fluids and egg stops for a time.

Menstruation has a psychological feature which is emotional irritability. Modern physicians tell us that this is traceable to decreased levels of estrogen and progesterone. This, however, is only part of the story. There is a parallel loss which occurs in the subtle form of mental and emotional psychic energy.

Chapter 20
Mandatory
Sexual Encounters

Our actions from past transmigrations served as impetus in the subtle energy. The impressions form manifestations and pull us into various circumstances. It may be compared to a man who committed a crime and then left for a distant place. As soon as he returns to the area in which the violence was perpetrated, the police may arrest him. The only way to avoid this is to remain at the distant place. Previous flirtations and sexual misbehaviors cause us to be drawn into new sexual temptations.

A certain minimal amount of sexual advances will have to be endured. These cannot be avoided. Merely by being in the gross or subtle environment one will be sexually attracted and one will be a sexual attraction. Even those who go to an isolated place, must deal with memories and sexual attractions on the subtle plane.

One should learn how to handle lust when it is directed to the self. One may receive it, without being affected. One may convert the energy back into a neutral emotion or one may release it back into the atmosphere. If one tries to avoid it altogether, it may increase in potency and draw one's attention in another way. It is best to take it, and adjust it. Then release it as raw energy without sexual content.

Sexual encounters which are forced on anyone must be dealt with in one way or another. One cannot avoid all of it. Circumstances of this nature are mandatory, destined meetings, which are enforced by providence.

An accomplished yogi is a very powerful individual but that does not mean that he could withstand all imposing circumstances. After all, he is limited. He must respect providence. One source of mandatory sexual encounter, is formulated romances from a past life. If an ascetic is on the subtle plane or on the gross and subtle simultaneously, he will have to deal with some reactions of past romances. He will have to retrieve the sexual energies which were emitted from his psyche in some past life. These sexual powers which might be lodged in the subtle bodies of others, would have to be carefully recalled. And this mystic act of retrieval should be performed carefully, in a way that does not initiate further contact.

All deep romances and unfulfilled loves from previous lusty encounters from many previous lives, cannot be solved out unless one resorts to mystic process. If one attempts to settle this physically, it would mean endless social complications.

Chapter 21
Mystic Sex

When religious people hear about mystic sex, some try to deny it while others simply shun such conversations, thinking that such discussions are below their dignity. We ought to understand that unless we have mystic vision we are, more than likely, indulging in mystic sex. Unless a human being can remember every dream clearly, we can know for certain that the denial of mystic sex and the avoidance of philosophical conversations of it, is a type of hypocrisy.

Mystic sex is real. In fact, it is more real than gross indulgence. The subtle senses are much more active, forceful and permissive than the gross ones.

Psychic semen

The subtle body has sexual organs. Subtle sexual hormones flow through those organs. Once I saw some astral beings in sexual embrace. With subtle sight, one may see psychic semen flowing from a subtle penis into a subtle vagina.

While in the physical body, the liquid semen passes out of the body through a tiny opening in the male organ. In the astral body, the semen passes through tiny tubes which perforate the head of the organ.

We experience the subtle body while using the gross one. Usually we do not sort the gross and the subtle ones. In a gross intercourse, the semen flows through the tiny tube in the head of the organ but the sexual pleasure passes through the entire head. In fact, the sexual pleasure begins within the body in the region of the pubococcygeus muscle.

During a gross intercourse, the subtle body is involved. But in the astral world, there is no gross body, only the subtle one. The intercourse there is much more intense since the grossness or resistance of the gross body is absent. Subtle female bodies draw energy through a sucking ring in the entrance to the vaginal passage. This sucking ring acts like a vacuum draw.

sex you!

A sexual energy head passage

One can transit disembodied souls through the back of the head of the subtle body, thus getting rid of them when they entered to motivate for sexual intercourse.

In this procedure, the entities enter the kundalini central passage in the spine. This is called the central sushumna passage. Once there, they moved up and out through a brilliant light that goes out through the head of the astral body. There is a wonderful effect of an energized subtle body, in that the entities become divested of lusty force as they pass through the light of subtle form. However after exiting, their subtle bodies resume the lusty energy and they seek out another parent.

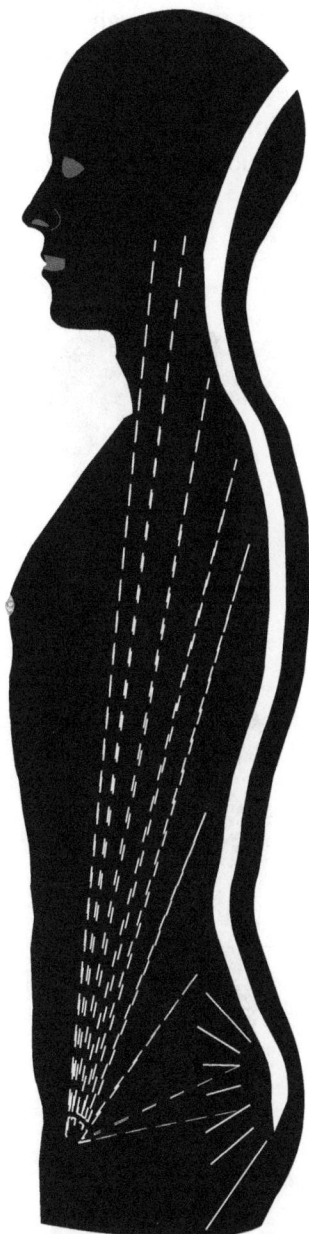

There is another passage through which some leave the body of a man who is reluctant to have intercourse. Sometimes they leave through a tiny hole at the base of the subtle spine. Some leave through the navel. Others burst out from the subtle chest. But the most used exit is the sexual organ.

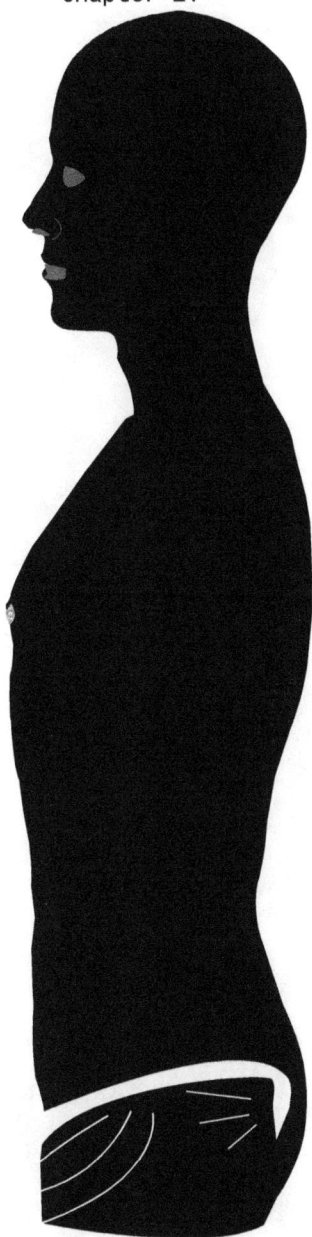

sex you!

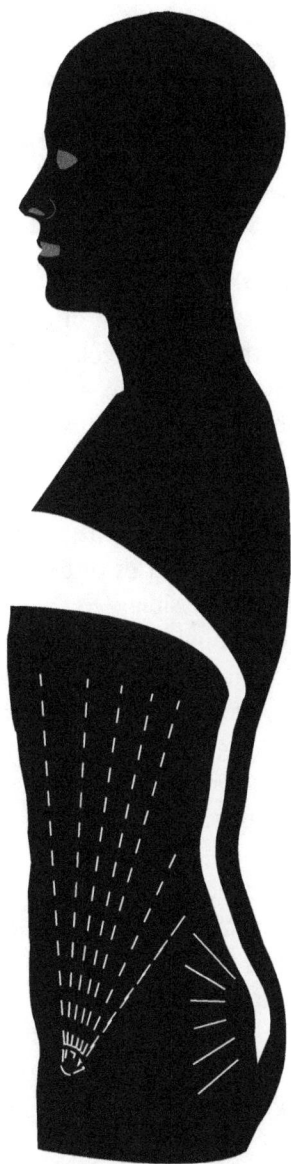

Chapter 22:
Sexual Expression:
Causal Plane

Sexual desire on the causal plane manifests only as a desire to experience the psyche of another. There are no sexual entries on the causal level, even though souls who are affectionately matched, do enter in and out of each other's causal bodies. In these causal love acts, organs are not involved but rather the whole person with psychological energies, enters the causal form of the other person. On the causal level, neither organs nor limbs are manifested. The sexual entries of the type we know in an earthly body, are not possible.

The causal level though free of action, is filled with desires. The whole realm is saturated with potent psychic energy. When a yogi gets to the causal plane after eliminating sexual urges on the gross and subtle levels, he must consider attachment to desires. Usually the advanced yogis are left with two types of social desires. The first has to do with assisting others with their liberation. The second has to do with specific focus on certain entities who are spiritually connected.

A yogi who reaches the causal plane might again return to deal with sexual desires but these desires are not his own. These are the desires of others who desire his association but who are not freed from the urge. If he has to help them, he will have to assume some primitive tendencies in their association. He will then be required to purify himself and encourage his spiritual dependents to take reforming disciplines.

Some great yogis who come down from the causal plane become stranded on a lower level for a time. This is due to their effort to reform specific souls or the general public. If they become stalled, they eventually realize it, and again turn away from the world, using strict austerities to escape to the causal level.

The general public cannot be freed by any limited yogi no matter how powerful he may be. They can only be freed by a divinity. Generally the divine person enlists the service of others in salvation attempts. The responsibility of elevating the masses is given to several spiritual masters. Even the power-house spiritual masters like Jesus Christ work through others. These powerful supernaturals are able to elevate many living entities but even they sublet their powers to others and divide the work of salvation among assistants.

To be singled out for salvation is a wonderful thing for any living entity. Indeed, unless one is singled out, the hope for liberation is a fantasy only. Those freed but limited yogis, who are assigned to free one or two souls, do meet with resistance in their task. In as much as an ant has a challenge in hauling a twig across a jungle floor, so these yogis have their headaches trying to free one or two souls. The task is sufficient for them.

When all is said and done, sexual desire is the greatest challenge in the quest for sense control. And once we complete abstinence, we have to deal with the sexual desire of those whose spiritual development is our responsibility. Thus, once we reach the causal plane we become stranded again as our spiritual advancement becomes checked when a divine being insists that we do more teaching on lower levels.

One of my spiritual masters, Mahayogin Yogesh, explained this situation. He said:

"I repeatedly reached the causal level and went into the

clean psychic energy there but I find that repeatedly my psyche is transferred from there. Some great yogis stay there for the entire duration of the universe which is billions of years. And then, when the creation fizzes out, they enter the undifferentiated spiritual energy. Then again we come back out when the universe is manifested. The God of the creation produces the world by His proximity to psychic material nature. He does not directly engineer the cosmos. There are many subagents."

It is definite, therefore, from this experience of the great yogi, that once we master sexual expression and we are done with lust, we must satisfy both ourselves and the divinities by working for the elevation of others. While doing this, our spiritual limbs and senses might manifest, according to our status in relation to a divine being. And then we may go to spiritual dimensions. Otherwise, ideas of salvation are pretty much a fantasy.

Description of the causal body

Yogesh wanted me to divulge that information and some related diagrams. Two tubes emerge from the causal body. One goes upwards and the other goes downwards. From these, the subtle body is created. The upward tube extends to form the mind which, later on, forms the basis for the creation of the brain. The tube going downward, forms the life force which, later on, forms the spine. The physical heart is an extension of one of the chakras or energy gyrating centers for physical distribution of the life force.

sex you!

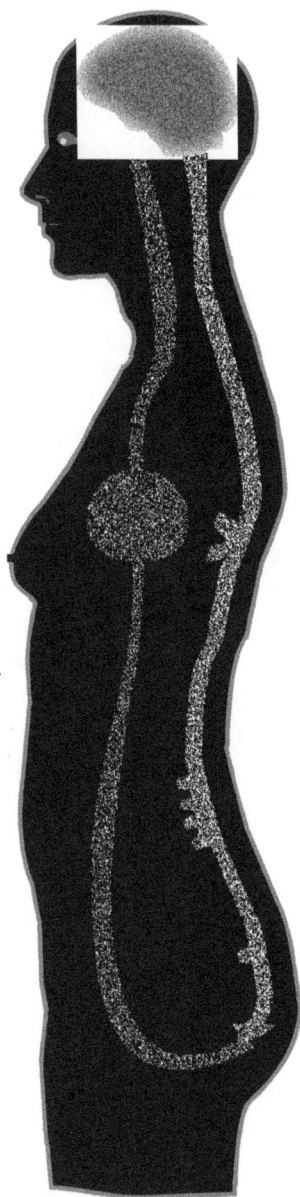

In the hatha yoga manuals like the *Shiva Samhita*, the *Gherananda Samhita* and the *Hatha Yoga Pradipika*, as well as in Lord Krishna's instructions to Uddhava*, the tubes of the subtle body are described and the causal body is indicated.

Mystic procedures

There are many mystic actions in hatha yoga, pranayama and tantric yoga practice. These processes are efficient techniques for achieving certain aims in physical, psychic and causal disciplines. The causal level is the level of ideation, the level of subjective subtle thinking. Higher than the causal plane, is the plane of the highest psychic mundane energy. Beyond that, there is the level of undifferentiated spiritual energy.

I will explain a few techniques and give credit to the yogis who introduced these. Some years ago, when I lacked confidence that my black body could attain regulated sexual expression, Swami Shivananda assured me that it was possible by consistent practice. He said,

> *"I know for a fact that any human body can become sexually-resistant if given the proper treatment of postures, diet and breath practice."*

Later on he was to tell me that the secret of sexual expression lay in keeping the seminal tubes dry of semen. In the beginning one has to arrange the diet so that one does not take excess liquids in the late afternoon or at night. This initial practice gives just a little result but it is important. If there are liquids in the stomach in the late afternoon and at night, there will be urine in the bladder, liquid will flow in the testes and motivate indulgence.

Uddhava Gītā Explained: **ISBN 978-0-9819332-1-4**
Uddhava Gita English: **ISBN 978-0-9819332-0-7**

A special practice was shown to me by Swami Shivananda. The procedure is to draw up the semen to the heart chakra, using the bow posture with stress on the chest muscles.

Once the fluid begins to go there on a regular basis, one then pulls it into the neck channel and then at last into the brain. After this, one increases control of diet. One does not take a drop more of food or liquid than is required. Then one learns how to stretch the seminal tubes so that the system can act more efficiently to absorb semen into the bloodstream. One should learn how to get lust-free hormones into the seminal tubes so as to reduce and cancel out the lusty sexual charge.

Muscles forming the pelvic base.

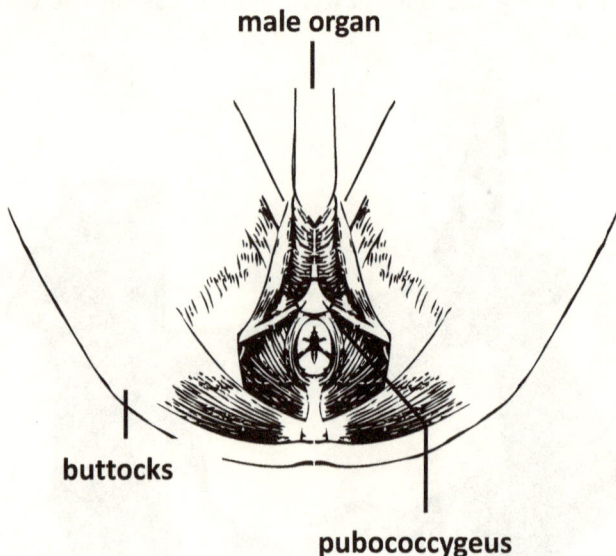

male organ

buttocks

pubococcygeus

Contraction of the pubococcygeus muscle was explained by Swami Satyananda. This muscle is the one that triggers the intense pleasure of sexual climax. The self-tantric yogi is not concerned with orgasm but with controlling this muscle and directing the semen away from the organ. In some Oriental tantric practices, this pubococcygeus muscle is manipulated for sexual pleasure but this yogic sexual restraint aims at the opposite effect, which is sublimation of the sexual urge.

Apart from the standard vajroli, Satyananda showed me another. In this practice, one takes in any sexual energy that comes to one's body because of a former romance. This refers to mandatory sexual encounters. One takes in the energy, since one cannot avoid it. One pulls it into the causal heart space. Most of this occurs on the psychic level.

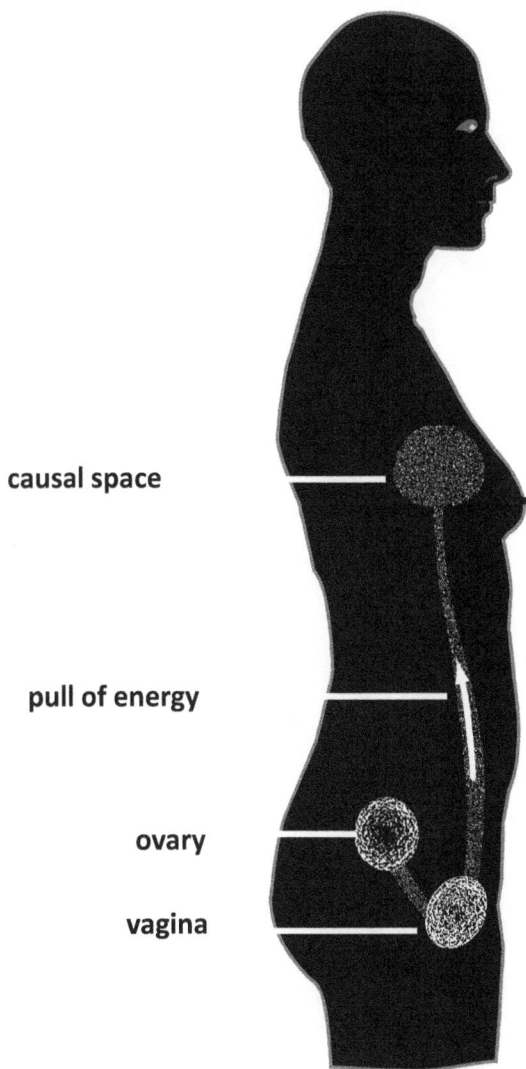

causal space

pull of energy

ovary

vagina

sex you!

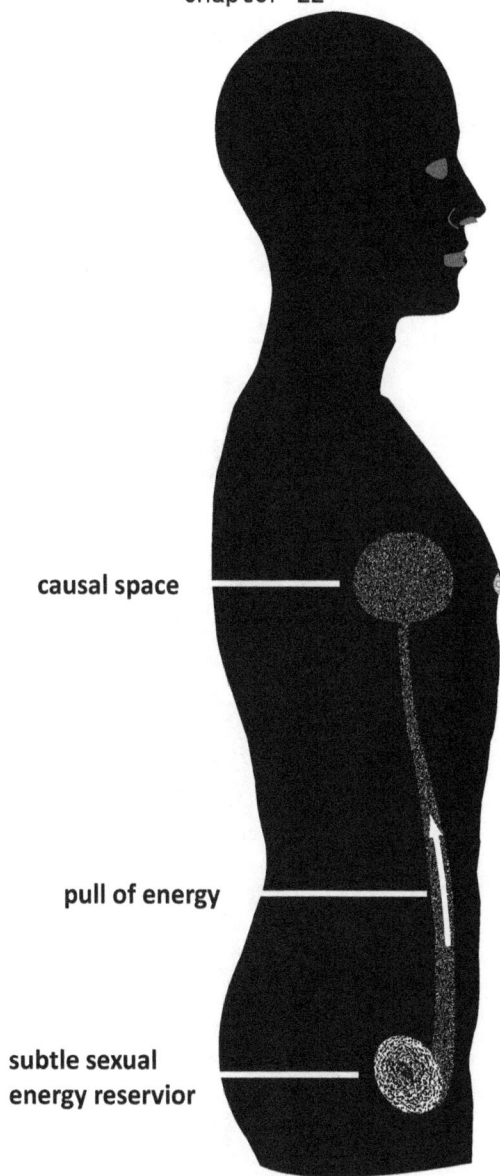

causal space

pull of energy

subtle sexual
energy reservior

sex you!

Closing the sexual intercourse chakra

The sex chakra which radiates from the spine is entirely different to the sexual intercourse chakra. The diagram below shows the major spinal chakras. More diagrams follow, which differentiate the sexual intercourse chakra.

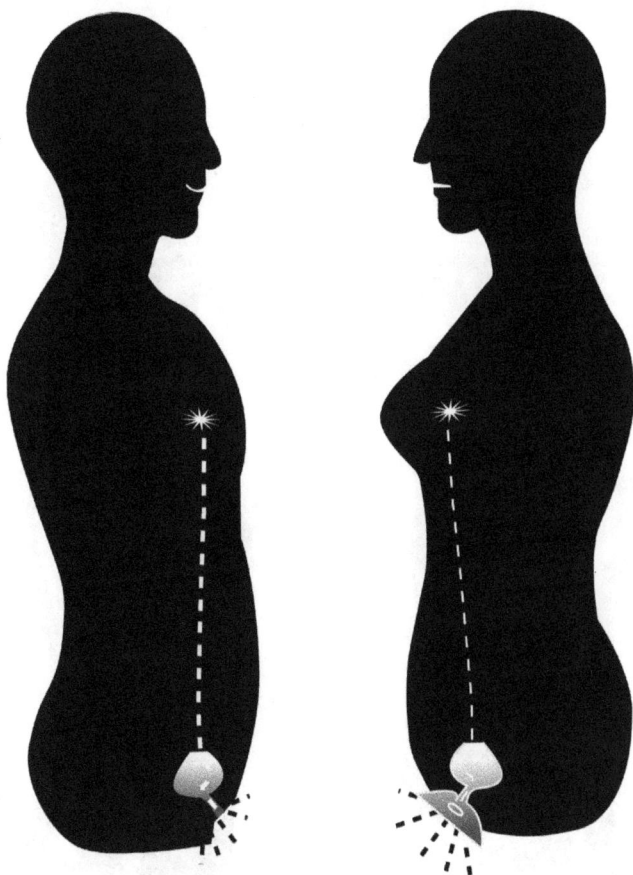

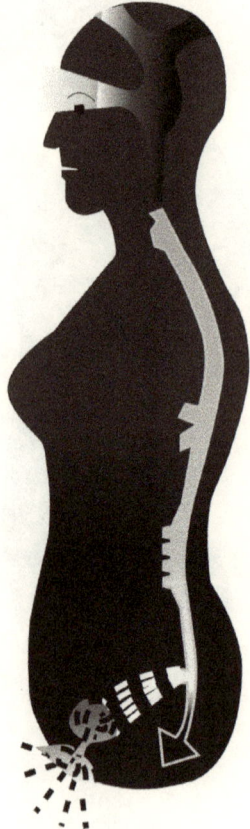

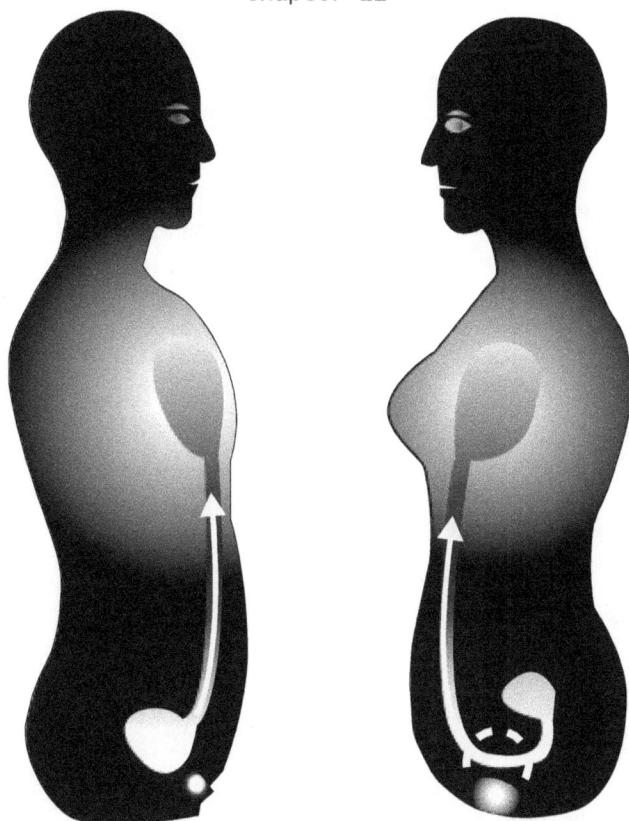

- *Basic communication between causal cove and reproductive system*

sex you!

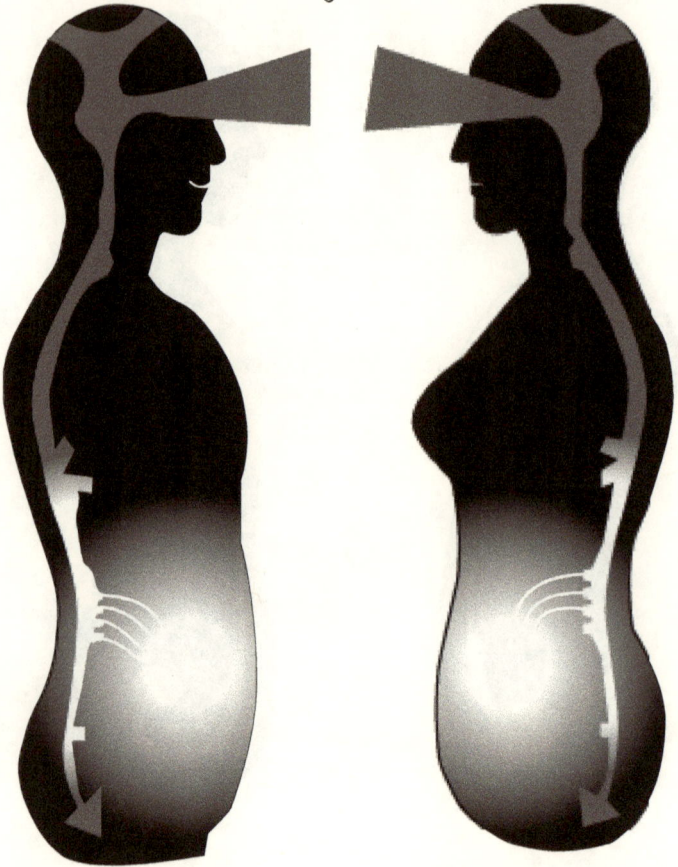

- *Communication between life force and digestive mechanisms*

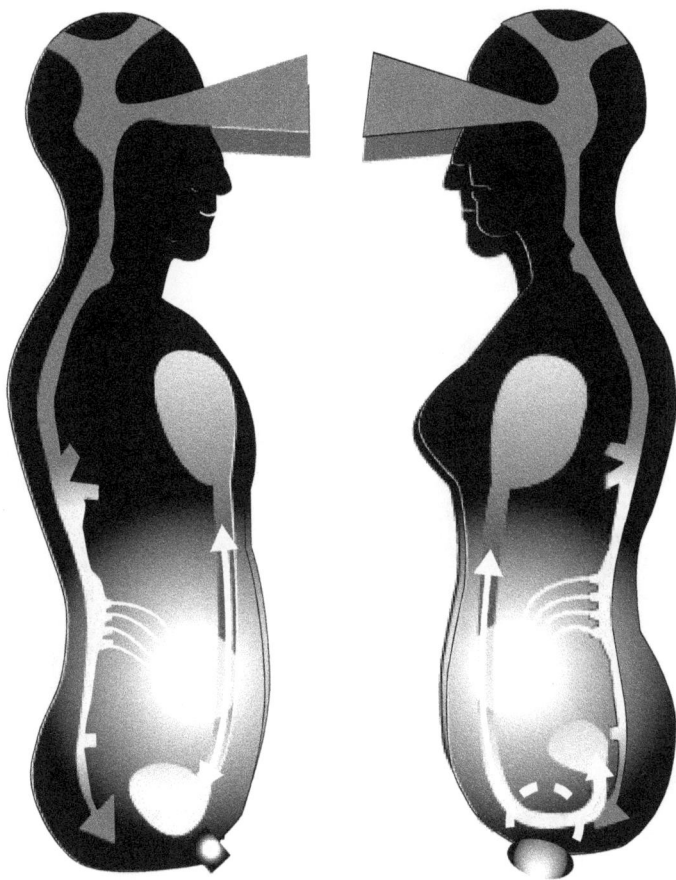

- *Communication between energized digestive mechanisms and linked causal and reproductive systems*

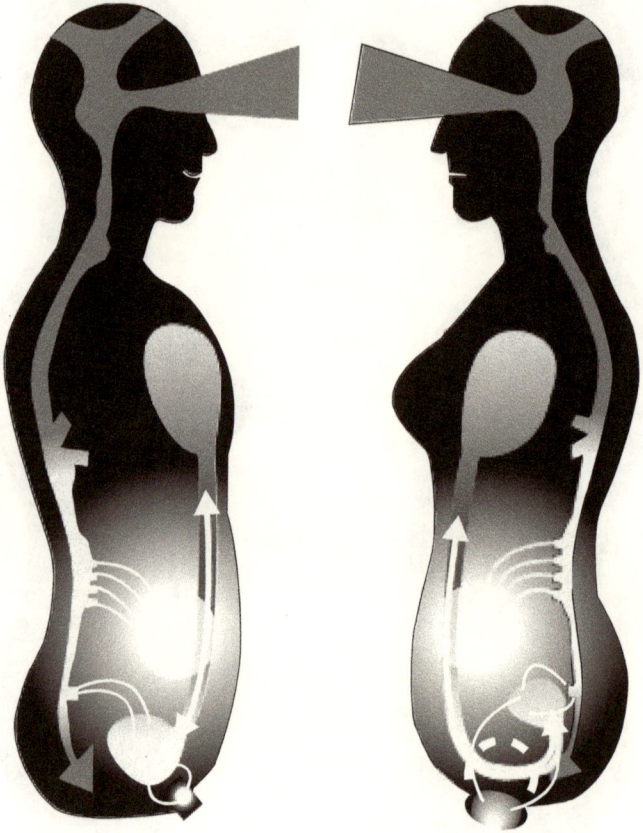

- *Digestive and reproductive systems fully energised by life force and causal energy*

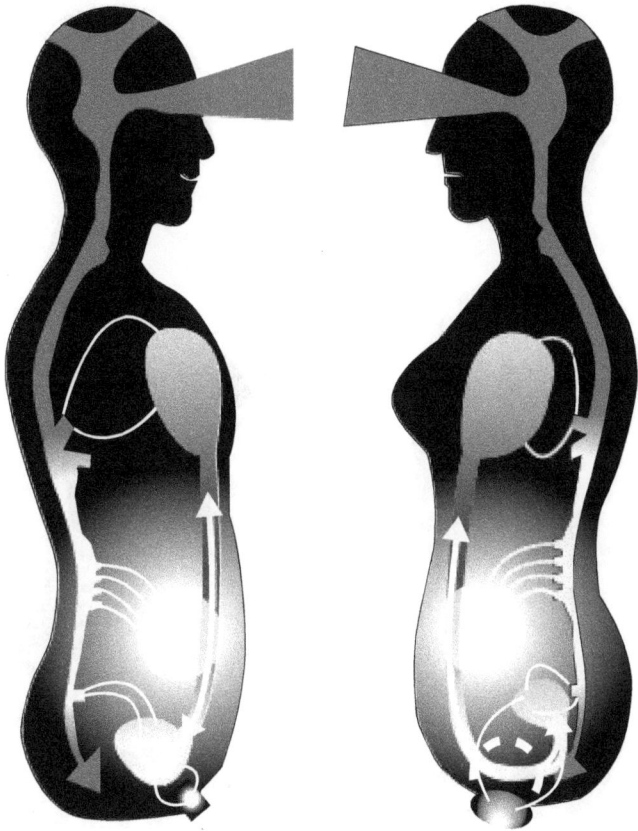

- *Causal energy linked to life force system*

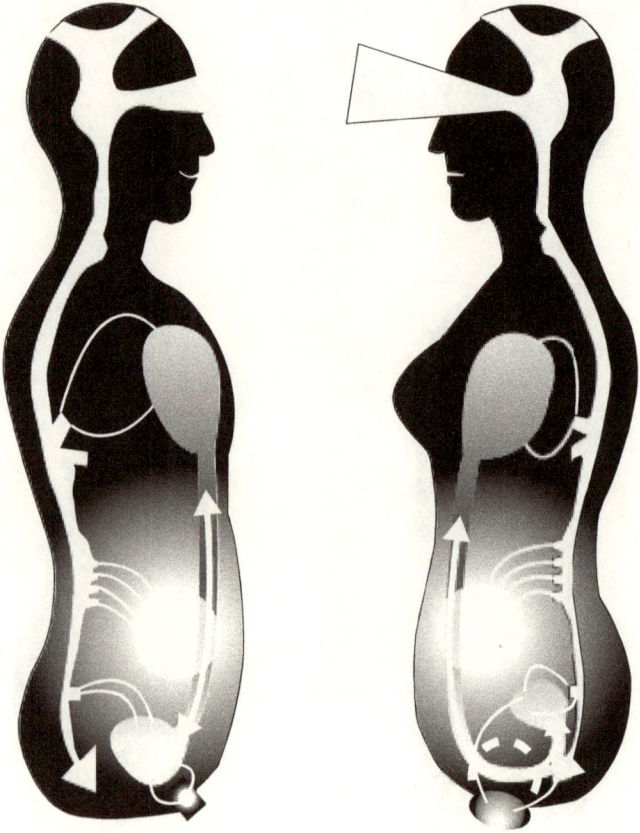

- *Life force system activated in head of body*
- *Causal energy unconnected to head*

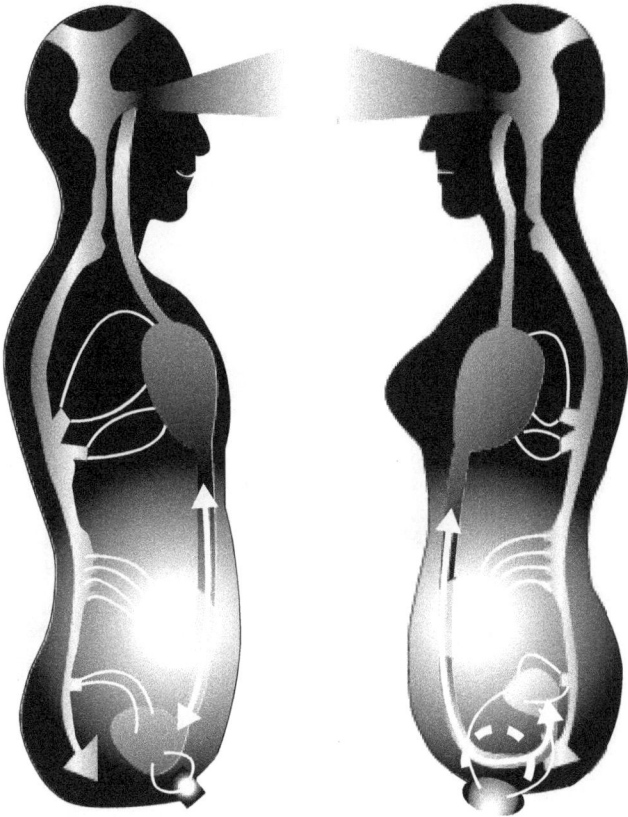

- *Life force system and causal energy flowing in head*

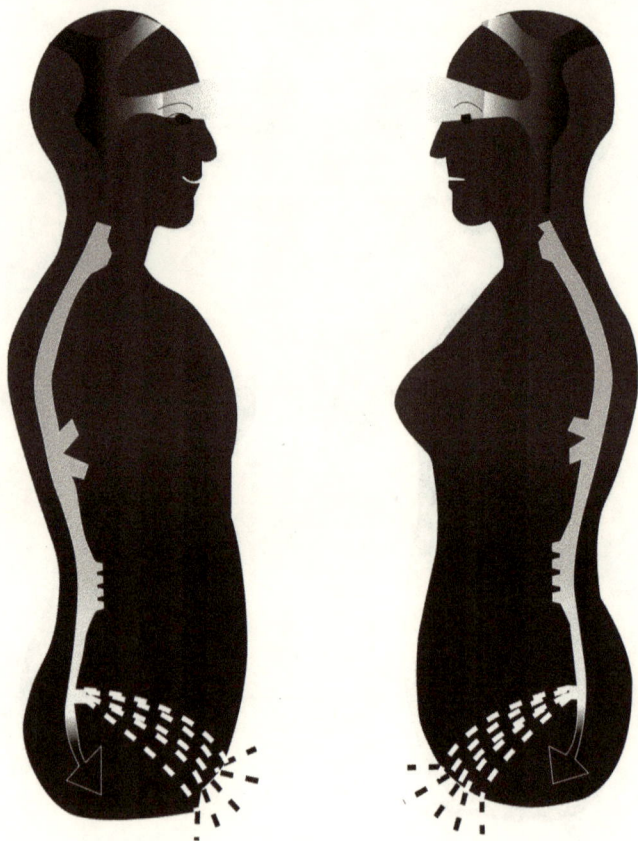

- *During a sexual exchange, the focus of the sex chakra is the sexual organs.*

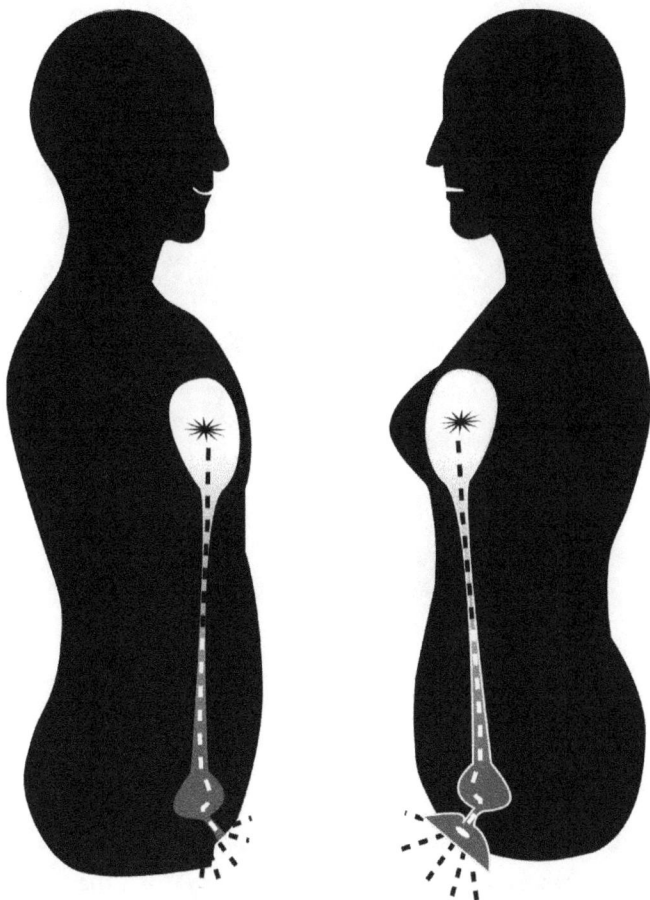

- *A tube extends downward from the causal space to a sexual reservoir which empties into the sexual intercourse chakra.*

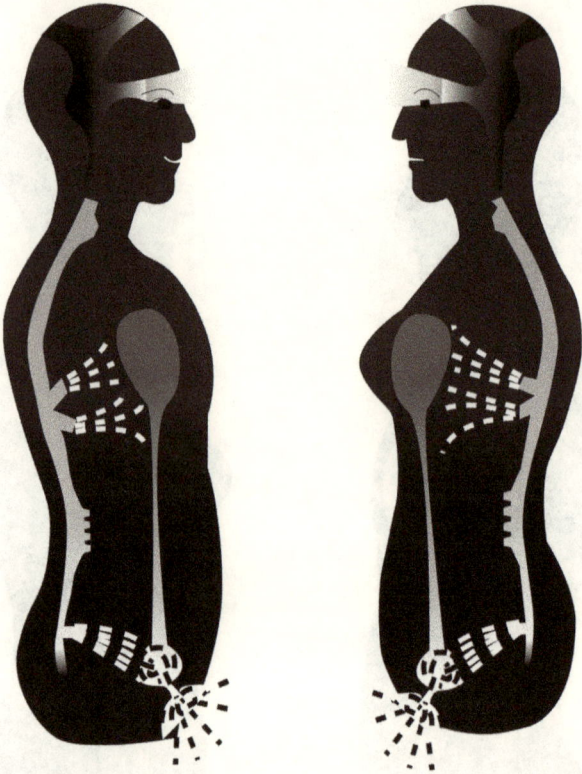

- *Sexual energy funnels downward through the reservoir. The lower opening of the male reservoir is narrower.*

- *From its position in the causal heart, the soul peers down the causal heart tube all the way through the sexual reservoir opening*

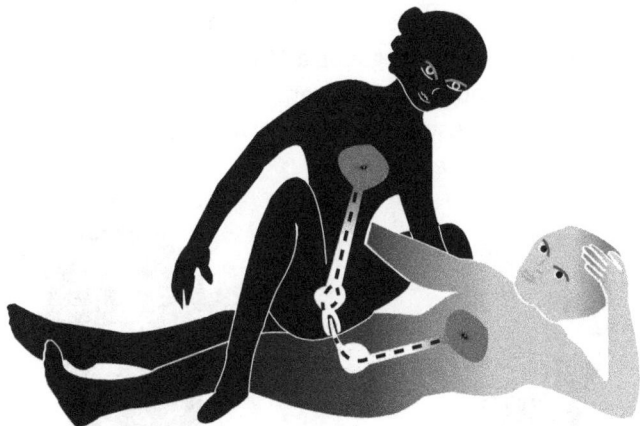

- *This is the perspective of the subtle energy and forms during a gross sexual intercourse of a tantric yogi and yogini.*

The sex chakra operates to generate sexual fluids and to facilitate and channel hormones and romantic energies but the sexual intercourse chakra lies dormant until an orgasm or sexual pleasure experience becomes intensified. Once it is intensified this chakra opens up fully and overpowers the entire body. The power of this chakra has nearly everyone craving sexual indulgence. In yoga practice, this chakra is retracted by withdrawing it into the sex chakra on the spine and into the bottom of the causal heart space.

Two yogis of repute, Satyananda and Yogesh, are responsible for showing me how this chakra developed

sex you!

from the causal form and how it is withdrawn by the expert yogis who are done with lust on the gross and psychic planes.

Just two months before this book went to publication, I found myself in a subtle dimension, a parallel world which is controlled by Sri Nisargadatta Maharaja (1897-1981). He directed me to put these diagrams in this book.

These concern those beings who have a subtle body which has no sexual interest.

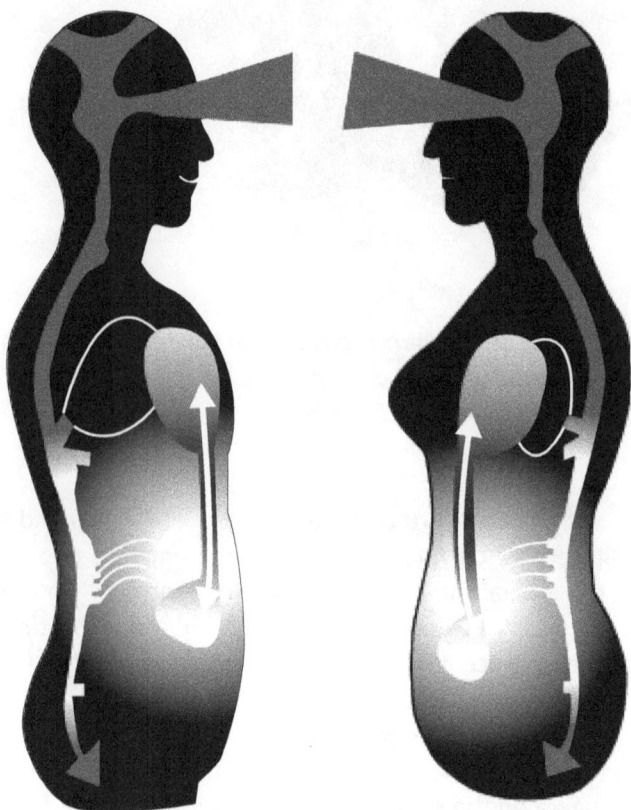

- *Sex chakra and mechanisms de-activated*
- *Causal energy system descends only as low as navel region*

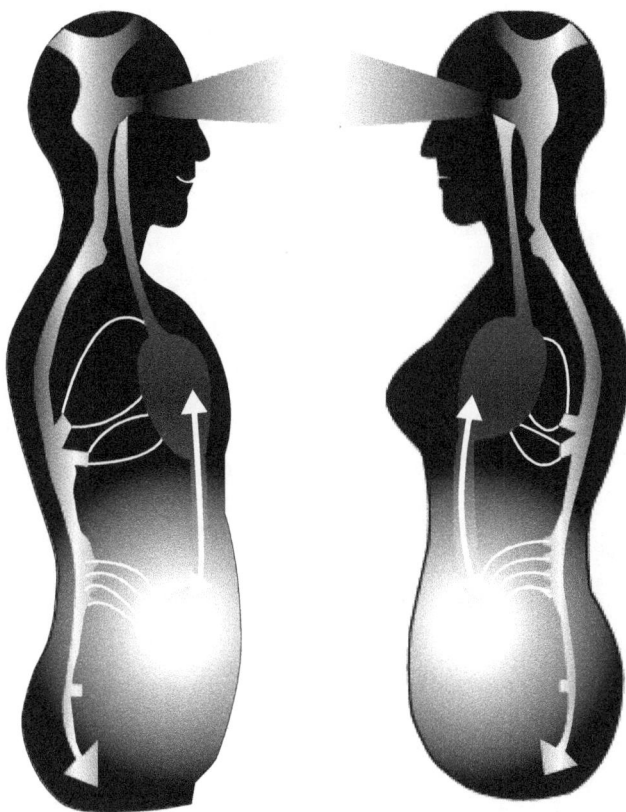

- *Spinal life force and causal body operating without sexual chakra input*

Index

I

idea, 72
ideation, 221
Ila, 122, 123
ill health, 49
imagination, 177
implanter, 10
impotence, 75
impulses, 147
impulsion, 166
impulsiveness, 136
incongruency, 101
inconsistency, 139
indentation, 37
Indra, 105
indulgence
    criminal, 36
    drive increases, 146
    force, 77
    impulsion, 166
    restraint, 150
    sweetness, 136
infant,
    gender, 194
    helpless, 190
    organ attachment, 141
insight, 29, 30,
instinct, 122
intellect, 48
intellectual community, 47
intercourse,
    -see sexual intercourse
intestines, 63, 152
item, psychological, 26

J, K

Jarat, 21
Jesus Christ, 216
justifications, 77

juveniles, 140
Kardama, 87
kidney failure, 49
kisses, 73
Krishna, 15, 102, 221
Krishna deity, 195
Kubera, 118
kundalini, 18, 45, 153, 209
kundalini surge, 58

L

lactation, 166
lap, 141
laziness, 170
ledge, 21
lesbian,
    activities, 127
    cause, 134
    dominant one, 128
    relations, 120
life force,
    assisted, 167
    composition, 98
    defined, 18-19
    duties, 177, 180
    enjoyment, 76
    escape, 180
    fight, 152
    location, 49, 184
    organ control, 152
    sex forms, 54
    sex inclined, 48
    sex opportunity, 73
    sexual expression, 9
    surge, 58
liquid diet, 221
liquor, 66, 162
loss of confidence, 151
love, 197

V

vagina,
component, 198
cream, 26
secretions, 136
subtle, 206, 208
vajroli, 196-197, 223
valium, 66
Vasisht, 122
vernal equinox, 160
vibrators, 130
Vichitra, 128
victimizations, 73
video, 135, 145
Virat, 81
virus, 72
vow, 137
vulgar sexual entries, 150
vulgarity, 30, 120

W

waist, 37
wealthy parents, 72
weather cools, 158
wedlock, 29
weeds, 149

weights, 126
wet dream, 79, 176
white-skinned body, 43
whole person, 145
wife, 41, 139
woman,
aggressive type, 130
body nourishment, 193
entrapment, 146
menstruation, 91, 203
organ invigorated, 147
pleasure nerves, 112, 148
womb, outside, 26
work out, 126

Y

Yogesh, 216-217, 237
yogi,
causal plane, 215
dependents, 215
escape, 216
limited, 205
stranded, 216
young man, 154
young woman, 154

Glossary

Ajamil

Ajamil, a deviant devotee of Krishna (Vishnu) who was pardoned from hell hereafter by the agents of Vishnu.

Amba

A woman who took birth as a female baby in her next life and who then became a transsexual name Shikhand (Shikhandi). In the birth as Amba she was one of three sisters who were princesses. They were kidnapped by General Bhishma who intended to marry them to his brother Vichitra. Of the three sisters, this one, Amba refused to marry Vichitra. She was released by Bhishma but when he returned to her lover, he rejected her. Subsequently she performed austerities with intentions of subduing Bhishma who also rejected her.

She was unable to take revenge in that life but the deity Shiva promised that in her next life she would be a man and would defeat Bhishma. By the grace of the deity this actually took place when she was born as a female named Shikhandini and then had a sex change and became Shikhand.

Arjuna

A warrior in the Kurukshetra war which is described in the Mahabharata. Arjuna became famous as the student of Krishna who was instructed in the Bhagavad Gita.

He is mentioned in this book in relation to his feat of causing some angelic women to be released from reptilian profiles.

Bhagavad Gita

A discussion in the Mahabharata, which became famous as a separate literature. It is a philosophical and revelatory incidence between the lecturer who was Krishna and the inquirer who was Arjuna.

Bhajan, Yogi

-See Yogi Bhajan in this listing.

Bhishma

> The heroic grandsire of the Kuru dynasty. He vouched that Krishna was the God Vishnu. He stated that Krishna and Arjuna came previously as the deities Nara-Narayana. He was rated as being eternally liberated. He took the course of the sun during its ascendency to the Northern Hemisphere in order to use it to reach higher dimensions. Once during the battle of Kurukshetra, Krishna took up a chariot wheel to kill Bhishma's body but Arjuna stopped Krishna by pledging that he would kill Bhishma, who was in fact his great-uncle, but who has supported corrupt members of the Kuru family.

Budha

> The person who was the husband of Ila, the androgyne transgender

Devahuti

> This Princess was the wife of Kardama a proficient yogi devotee of Krishna. Devahuti, who was a proficient yogini, was imparted transcendental experience by her son Kapila, who is rated as a divine personality.

Drupad

> A king who was humbled by Drona. They were friends in school and Drupad promised to give half of his ancestral lands to Drona but later denied the promise. Drona used the Kuru princes to subdue Drupad. Drona then took half of Drupad's ancestral territory. The result was Drona's death by Drupad's son during the Battle of Kurukshetra.

Duryodhana

> The villain of the Mahābhārata. He was a cousin of Arjuna. Even though he was shown the Universal Form of Krishna in an apparition which scared most persons who saw it, he dismissed Krishna as a mere magician.

Himalayas

> The highest mountain range in the world, located in Northern India. It is pronounced as Him-ah-lay uh, instead of Him-uh-lay-uh

Hiranyavarna

After being informed that Shikhandin was female, this legendary king marched against King Manu. He felt disgraced since Manu had successfully proposed that Shikhandin should marry the daughter of Hiranyavarna.

Ila

She was the female self of the male person known as Shudyu.

Kardama

A legendary and very accomplished yogi, who was the husband of the divine lady known as Devahuti. Kardama was a devotee of Krishna. During his amorous affairs with Devahuti, he managed to split himself in 9 persons of himself and conducted sexual affairs with his wife in that way.

Krishna

This person portrayed himself as the Supreme Person to Arjuna. His declarations and the supporting evidence are given in the Mahābhārata and the Srimad Bhagavatam (Bhagavata Purana).

Krishna became famous mainly through his discourse with Arjuna before the battle of Kurukshetra. This conversation is part of the Mahābhārata literature but it is presented as a book in its own right under the title of Bhagavad Gītā.

Kubera

A supernatural being who regulates human usage of valuable resources,

kundalini

The physio-subtle life support system which operates on its own to maintain a living body. It has the tendency for survival and protects the body regardless of the interest or disinterest of the soul person who uses the body.

Mahābhārata

As a word, this means the Great Legends of India (Bharata). This book is the biography of the Kauravas, the Kuru dynasty, but it has many other literatures within it. It proclaims that if something cannot be found in it, such a thing does not exist anywhere.

Manu

This ancient king was the father of Shudyu, After being
petitioned by Manu, the mystic priest Vasisht changed the
gender of the child to that of a male but later that was
reversed through enchantment by Shiva and Durga. But
after this reversal, Vasisht managed to appease Shiva and
caused Shudyu be a genuine transgender, changing from
male to female and visa versa on a monthly basis.

Parshram

An ancient warrior teacher who was rated as a divine
being. He taught military tactics to Bhishma. When
Princess Amba asked Parshram to subdue Bhishma, the
teacher failed in the attempt.

Puran

Puran (Puranjana) was a fictional king. His allegoric story
was told by Narada to King Prachina-barhi. At first the
king thought that Puran was really an historic personality
but when he asked about the lineage, Narad explained that
Puran represented the soul person who uses material
bodies.

Satyananda

This was a yogi guru. He was a disciple of Swami
Shivananda. The special feature of this Swami was his
adherence to the sannyasa order for not taking disciples
and privileges and not maintaining preaching missions in
the sannyasa order.

Shikhand

This person was a transgender, but in the past life was
Princess Amba. Due to desire and the approval of the Shiva
deity, she took a male sexual aspect in the life as
Shikhandini. Thus she became known as Shikhandi which is
a male name.

Her purpose for that life was to take revenge on General
Bhishma who kidnapped her in the previous life and
frustrated her marriage destiny.

Her past life and new reincarnation was known to
Bhishma. When before the battle of Kurukshetra, General
Bhishma declared that he would not kill a woman or

anyone who was once a woman, Duryodhana inquired about that objection. Bhishma then explained Shikhand's past life and her resentment towards him for frustrating her romantic life.

Shikhandin was not skilled enough to kill Bhishma but he succeeded in acting as shield for Arjuna who shadowed behind him on the battlefield and took Bhishma down.

Shiva

Shiva is considered to be one of the three primal deities in the Hindu Pantheon of Deities. The other two are Brahma and Vishnu.

In the Shiva Purana, Shiva is presented as the Supreme Being over all other deities in the Vedic Pantheon.

His wife is Devi, Durga, the Woman God.

Shivananda

A celibate yogi monk, who established the divine life society. He is a Mahayogin.

Sudyu

The son of King Manu. Because of secret incantations, this person was born female. On request of the father to a mystic priest named Vasisht, the child's was transgendered. However later on in life, the transgender experienced a reversal and again assumed a female profile.

This was because of a curst placed on a forest which was own by Goddess Durga. Due to interference to their privacy, Shiva cursed the place such that any male entering the region would instantly experience a sex change into a female.

However Sudyu got some blessings and was able to assume both male and female gender alternately each month, as Prince Sudyu and as Princess Ila. As that Princess she fell in love with Budha and had a child for him.

Stuna

Stuna was a sub-supernatural being who had magical powers and who could fulfill many desires instantly. He aided Shikhand who was born female to experience life as a transgender. This is described in the Mahābhārata

Upanishad

The Upanishads are a set of writings by some ancient yogi sages, whose ideas which are echoed in the Bhagavad Gita.

Vasisht

This person was an ancient priest and Vedic holy man with legendary powers. He managed to expedite the sex change of Ila the daughter of Manu. After becoming a male, that princess became known as Prince Sudyu.

Vichitra

This king was the younger of two sons of King Shantanu and Queen Satyavati. His paternal half-brother and elder was Bhishma who supervised everything during Vichitra's reign. Bhishma kidnapped three princesses and offered them to Vichitra, but one of the ladies, Amba, rejected the proposal.

Vichitra had no children and after his demise, by the request of their mother, his maternal half brother, a wise man known as Vyasa, sired three sons in the royal household on his behalf.

Yogesh

Yogeshwarananda Vyasji Mahayogin. This person is a dear spiritual master of the writer. Yogeshwarananda wrote many books, one of which is Science of the Soul.

The author cannot in any way repay him for the techniques he reveals on the astral plane.

Yogi Bhajan

This is a kundalini yoga master, from whom the writer learned the bhastrika pranayama method of kundalini yoga. This is a rapid method for causing kundalini to be cooperative with one's spiritual aspirations.

Yogiji established the 3HO Foundation during the life of his recent body. He is now departed but the writer keeps in contact with him on the astral planes.

Author

Michael Beloved (Madhvacharya das) took his current body in 1951 in Guyana. In 1965, while living in Trinidad, he instinctively began doing yoga postures and trying to make sense of the supernatural side of life.

Later on, in 1970, in the Philippines, he approached a Martial Arts Master named Mr. Arthur Beverford, explaining to the teacher that he was seeking a yoga instructor. Mr. Beverford identified himself as an advanced disciple of Sri Rishi Singh Gherwal, an ashtanga yoga master.

Mr. Beverford taught the traditional ashtanga yoga with stress on postures, attentive breathing and brow chakra centering meditation. In 1972, Michael entered the Denver Colorado Ashram of Kundalini Yoga Master Sri Harbhajan Singh. There he took instruction in Bhastrika Pranayama and its application to yoga postures. He was supervised mostly by Yogi Bhajan's disciple named Prem Kaur.

In 1979 Michael formally entered the disciplic succession of the Brahma-Madhva Gaudiya Sampradaya through Swami Kirtanananda, who was a prominent sannyasi disciple of the Great Vaishnava Authority Sri Swami Bhaktivedanta Prabhupada, the exponent of devotion to Sri Krishna.

Apart from this, Michael took instructions from proficient gurus on the astral planes. For producing this publication, Michael studied the psychic side of human existence and took guidance from reliable mystics and spiritual manuals which describe the course of reincarnation.

sex you!

Publications

English Series

Bhagavad Gita English

Anu Gita English

Markandeya Samasya English

Yoga Sutras English

Uddhava Gita English

These are in 21st Century English, very precise and exacting. Many Sanskrit words which were considered untranslatable into a Western language are rendered in precise, expressive and modern English, due to the English language becoming the world's universal means of concept conveyance.

Three of these books are instructions from Krishna. **In Bhagavad Gita English** and **Anu Gita English**, the instructions were for Arjuna. In the **Uddhava Gita English,** it was for Uddhava. Bhagavad Gita and Anu Gita are extracted from the Mahabharata. Uddhava Gita was extracted from the 11th Canto of the Srimad Bhagavatam (Bhagavata Purana). One of these books, the **Markandeya Samasya English** is about Krishna, as described by Yogi Markandeya, who survived the cosmic collapse and reached a divine child in whose transcendental body, the collapsed world was existing. Another of these books, the **Yoga Sutras English,** is the detailed syllabus about yoga practice.

My suggestion is that you read **Bhagavad Gita English**, the **Anu Gita English, the Markandeya Samasya English,** the **Yoga Sutras English** and lastly the **Uddhava Gita English**, which is much more complicated and detailed.

For each of these books we have at least one commentary, which is published separately. Thus your particular interest can be researched further in the commentaries.

The smallest of these commentaries and perhaps the simplest is the one for the Anu Gita. We published its commentary as the Anu Gita Explained. The Bhagavad Gita explanations were published in three distinct targeted commentaries. The first is Bhagavad Gita Explained, which sheds lights on how people in the time of Krishna and Arjuna regarded the information and applied it. Bhagavad Gita is an exposition of the application of yoga practice to cultural activities, which is known in the Sanskrit language as karma yoga.

Interestingly, Bhagavad Gita was spoken on a battlefield just before one of the greatest battles in the ancient world. A warrior, Arjuna, lost his wits and had no idea that he could apply his training in yoga to political dealings. Krishna, his charioteer, lectured on the spur of the moment to give Arjuna the skill of using yoga proficiency in cultural dealings including how to deal with corrupt officials on a battlefield.

The second commentary is the Kriya Yoga Bhagavad Gita. This clears the air about Krishna's information on the science of kriya yoga, showing that its techniques are clearly described free of charge to anyone who takes the time to read Bhagavad Gita. Kriya yoga concerns the battlefield which is the psyche of the living being. The internal war and the mental and emotional forces which are hostile to self-realization are dealt with in the kriya yoga practice.

The third commentary is the Brahma Yoga Bhagavad Gita. This shows what Krishna had to say outright and what he hinted about which concerns the brahma yoga practice, a mystic process for those who mastered kriya yoga.

There is one commentary for the **Markandeya Samasya English**. The title of that publication is Krishna Cosmic Body.

There are two commentaries to the Yoga Sutras. One is the Yoga Sutras of Patanjali and the other is the Meditation Expertise. These give detailed explanations of the process of Yoga.

For the Uddhava Gita, we published the Uddhava Gita Explained. This is a large book and requires concentration and study for integration of the information. Of the books which deal with transcendental topics, my opinion is that the discourse between Krishna and Uddhava has the complete information about the realities in existence. This book is the one which removes massive existential ignorance.

Meditation Series

Meditation Pictorial

Meditation Expertise

Core-Self Discovery

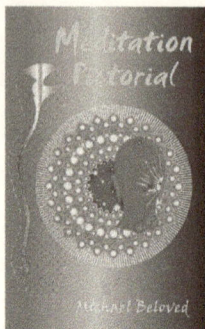

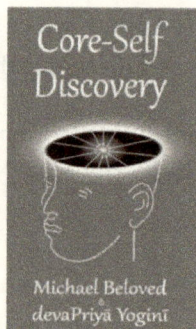

The specialty of these books is the mind diagrams which profusely illustrate what is written. This shows exactly what one has to do mentally to develop and then sustain a meditation practice.

In the **Meditation Pictorial**, one is shown how to develop psychic insight, a feature without which meditation is imagination and visualization, without any mystic experience per se.

In the **Meditation Experti**se, one is shown how to corral one's practice to bring it in line with the classic syllabus of yoga which Patanjali lays out as the ashtanga yoga eight-staged practice.

In **Core-Self Discovery**, one is taken though the course of pratyahar sensual energy withdrawal which is the 5th stage of yoga in the Patanjali ashtanga eight-process complete system of yoga practice. These events lead to the discovery of a core-self which is surrounded by psychic organs in the head of the subtle body. This product has a DVD component for teachers and self-teaching students.

These books are profusely illustrated with mind diagrams showing the components of psychic consciousness and the inner design of the subtle body.

Explained Series

Bhagavad Gita Explained

Uddhava Gita Explained

Anu Gita Explained

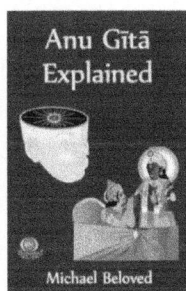

The specialty of these books is that they are free of missionary intentions, cult tactics and philosophical distortion. Instead of using these books to add credence to a philosophy, meditation process, belief or plea for followers, I spread the information out so that a reader can look through this literature and freely take or leave anything as desired.

When Krishna stressed himself as God, I stated that. When Krishna laid no claims for supremacy, I showed that. The reader is left to form an independent opinion about the validity of the information and the credibility of Krishna.

There is a difference in the discourse with Arjuna in the Bhagavad Gita and the one with Uddhava in the Uddhava Gita. In fact these two books may appear to contradict each other. In the Bhagavad Gita, Krishna pressured Arjuna to complete social duties. In the Uddhava Gita, Krishna insisted that Uddhava should abandon the same.

The Anu Gita is not as popular as the Bhagavad Gita but it is the conclusion of that text. Anu means what is to follow, what proceeds. In this discourse, an anxious Arjuna request that Krishna should repeat the Bhagavad Gita and again show His supernatural and divine forms.

However Krishna refuses to do so and chastises Arjuna for being a disappointment in forgetting what was revealed. Krishna then cites a celestial yogi, a near-perfected being, who explained the process of transmigration in vivid detail.

Commentaries

Yoga Sutras of Patanjali

Meditation Expertise

Krishna Cosmic Body

Anu Gita Explained

Bhagavad Gita Explained

Kriya Yoga Bhagavad Gita

Brahma Yoga Bhagavad Gita

Uddhava Gita Explained

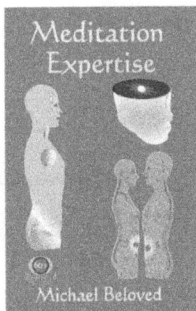

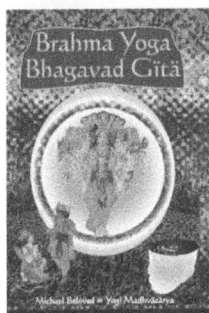

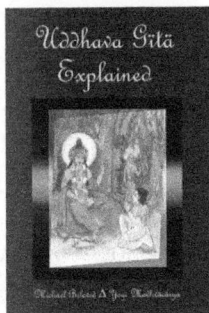

Yoga Sutras of Patanjali is the globally acclaimed text book of yoga. This has detailed expositions of yoga techniques. Many kriya techniques are vividly described in the commentary.

Meditation Expertise is an analysis and application of the Yoga Sutras. This book is loaded with illustrations and has detailed explanations of secretive advanced meditation techniques which are called kriyas in the Sanskrit language.

Krishna Cosmic Body is a narrative commentary on the Markandeya Samasya portion of the Aranyaka Parva of the Mahabharata. This is the detailed description of the dissolution of the world, as experienced by the great yogin Markandeya who transcended the cosmic deity, Brahma, and reached Brahma's source who is the divine infant, Krishna.

Anu Gita Explained is a detailed explanation of how we endure many material bodies in the course of transmigrating through various life-forms. This is a discourse between Krishna and Arjuna. Arjuna requested of Krishna a display of the Universal Form and a repeat narration of the Bhagavad Gita but Krishna declined and explained what a siddha perfected being told the Yadu family about the sequence of existences one endures and the systematic flow of those lives at the convenience of material nature.

Bhagavad Gita Explained shows what was said in the Gita without religious overtones and sectarian biases.

Kriya Yoga Bhagavad Gita shows the instructions for those who are doing kriya yoga.

Brahma Yoga Bhagavad Gita shows the instructions for those who are doing brahma yoga.

Uddhava Gita Explained shows the instructions to Uddhava which are more advanced than the ones given to Arjuna.

Bhagavad Gita is an instruction for applying the expertise of yoga in the cultural field. This is why the process taught to Arjuna is called karma yoga which means karma + yoga or cultural activities done with a yogic demeanor.

Uddhava Gita is an instruction for apply the expertise of yoga to attaining spiritual status. This is why it is explains jnana yoga and bhakti yoga in detail. Jnana yoga is using mystic skill for knowing the spiritual part of existence. Bhakti yoga is for developing affectionate relationships with divine beings.

Karma yoga is for negotiating the social concerns in the material world and therefore it is inferior to bhakti yoga which concerns negotiating the social concerns in the spiritual world.

This world has a social environment and the spiritual world has one too.

Right now Uddhava Gita is the most advanced informative spiritual book on the planet. There is nothing anywhere which is superior to it or which goes into so much detail as it. It verified that historically Krishna is the most advanced human being to ever have left literary instructions on this planet. Even Patanjali Yoga Sutras which I translated and gave an application for in my book, **Meditation Expertise**, does not go as far as the Uddhava Gita.

Some of the information of these two books is identical but while the Yoga Sutras are concerned with the personal spiritual emancipation (kaivalyam) of the individual spirits, the Uddhava Gita explains that and also explains the situations in the spiritual universes.

Bhagavad Gita is from the Mahabharata which is the history of the Pandavas. Arjuna, the student of the Gita, is one of the Pandavas brothers. He was in a social hassle and did not know how to apply yoga expertise to solve it. Krishna gave him a crash-course on the battlefield about that.

Uddhava Gita is from the Srimad Bhagavatam (Bhagavata Purana), which is a history of the incarnations of Krishna. Uddhava was a relative of Krishna. He was concerned about the situation of the deaths of many of his relatives but Krishna diverted Uddhava's attention to the practice of yoga for the purpose of successfully migrating to the spiritual environment.

Specialty

These books are based on the author's experiences in meditation, yoga practice and participation in spiritual groups:

Spiritual Master

sex you!

Sleep **Paralysis**

Astral Projection

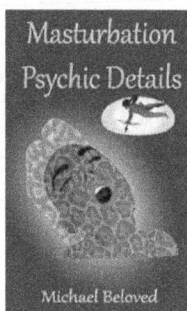

In **Spiritual Master**, Michael draws from experience with gurus or with their senior students. His contact with astral gurus is rated. He walks you through the avenue of gurus showing what you should do and what you should not do, so as to gain proficiency in whatever area of spirituality the guru has proficiency.

sex you! is a masterpiece about the adventures of an individual spirit's passage through the parents' psyches. The conversion of a departed soul into a sexual urge is described. The transit from the afterlife to residency in the emotions of the parents is detailed. This is about sex and you; learn about how much of you comprises the romantic energy of your would-be parents!

sex you!

Sleep Paralysis clears misconceptions so that one can see what sleep paralysis is and what frightening astral experience occurs while the paralysis is being experienced. This disempowerment has great value in giving you confidence that you can and do exist even if you are unable to operate the physical body. The implication is that one can exist apart from and will survive the loss of the material body.

Astral Projection details experiences Michael had even in childhood, where he assumed incorrectly that everyone was astrally conversant. He discusses the life force psychic mechanism which operates the sleep-wake cycle of the physical form, and which budgets energy into the separated astral form which determines if the individual will have dream recall or no objective awareness during the projections. Astral travel happens on every occasion when the physical body sleeps. What is missing in awareness is the observer status while the astral body is separated.

Masturbation Psychic Details is a surprise presentation which relates what happens on the psychic plane during a masturbation event. This does not tackle moral issues or even addictions but shows the involvement of memory and the sure but hidden subconscious mind which operates many features of the psyche irrespective of the desire or approval of the self-conscious personality.

Online Resources

Visit The Website And Forum

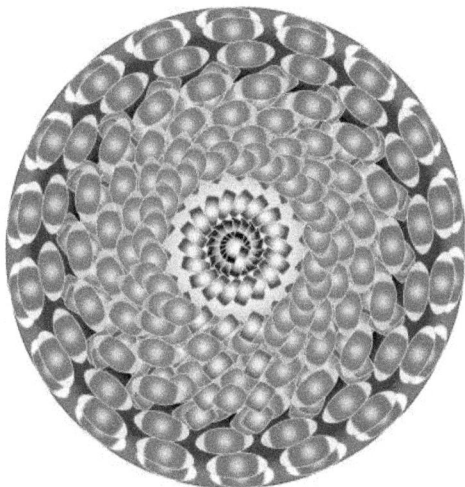

Email:	michaelbelovedbooks@gmail.com
	axisnexus@gmail.com

Website	michaelbeloved.com
Forum:	inselfyoga.com